MY TRAGIC PURSUIT AND THE 5 STEPS TO FREEDOM

Anthony Caputo

Copyright © Anthony Caputo 2019
The moral right of the author has been asserted.

Front cover and back cover photo by Sarah Stewart
Cover and layout design by Petya Tsankova

ISBN hardcover: 978-1-9990612-0-3
ISBN paperback: 978-1-9990612-2-7

All rights reserved. No part of this publication may be reproduced, stored in or introduced into a retrieval system, transmitted, in any form, or by any means (electronic, mechanical, photocopying, recording or otherwise) without the prior written consent of the publisher. Any person who does any unauthorised act in relation to this publication may be liable to criminal prosecution and civil claims for damages.

This book can be ordered from all bookstores, the author, and eplatforms such as Amazon.

Dedicated to my wife and kids who have always seen more in me than my mental illness and inspire me daily to achieve my dreams.
And to everyone out there struggling:
you all inspire me to continue
my mission of being a voice
for those that feel right now they can't.

TABLE OF CONTENTS

INTRODUCTION *to Part 1*	1
ANXIETY *Its Birth, Its Path of Destruction, and Its Death*	3
INTRODUCTION *to Part 2*	69
STEP ONE	73
STEP TWO	85
STEP THREE	93
STEP FOUR	101
STEP FIVE	107
CLOSING	113

INTRODUCTION
to Part 1

The dictionary describes an expert as a person who has comprehensive and authoritative knowledge or skill in a particular area. In my case, I became an expert in anxiety and depression. It wasn't by choice. Anxiety wrecked my life in lots of big ways and a zillion little ones. It reshaped my life, dictating choices, telling me what I could and couldn't do. It owned me. My life had some seriously horrible things in it that put anxiety in the driver's seat. I might have been highly anxious anyway but I definitely was after the massive heartaches and ugly situations I've gone through.

But greatness came out of it. I was able to come to an understanding of something of vital importance, something that the greatest minds have been trying to answer since the dawn of time. It is, in fact, the number one asked question on Google: What is the meaning of life?

It's funny because the only time that question has ever been answered is when people are on their deathbed. I was only ever living a half-life. Anxiety and depression stole the rest from me. And then it got worse. I've tasted death. Now I'm about to share with you the knowledge that I have acquired from being that close to it.

This book is divided into two halves. Throughout the first half of this book, I have woven little tasks. They might be simple. They might not be. They may open up some dark places inside you and if that's the case, then I apologize. Learning to a live a fuller life may not be entirely easy. When I was living with anxiety, I would have done anything, anything at all, to shift it. So these exercises are worth it.

In the second section, I offer steps that seem simple. I do them every day. Not joking. Every single day. I recommend that you do too. This book not only helps you overcome anxiety and depression, but it also shows you how to live a much fuller and deeper life. It gives you the tools you need to understand the meaning of your life. It will also help you achieve great success however you define it. Most say they want more money, but you can have something more precious: spiritually.

In order for you to understand the impact near death had on my life, I need to take you on a journey, my journey, to where it all started.

So here's my story, which is actually the story of my anxiety, from its birth through to its death.

I

ANXIETY

Its Birth, Its Path of Destruction, and Its Death

My journey started on a beautiful day in November 1977, the 16th to be exact, around 4:20 in the morning: my first day of life. I was born into a very loving and supportive family. My parents were young at the time but that didn't stop them from showering me with love or being the best possible parents they could.

I was born into an Italian family, the first born to both my parents and grandparents. In an Italian family that boils down to really one thing – being spoiled rotten. I was the highlight of my family's life; they called me the "golden child". Life was good. I had everything I could ask for as a child: parents who cared, and grandparents who spent every waking moment with me.

After I was born, I instantly developed a relationship with my grandfather. In fact, he was the one who carried me home from the hospital while my mother recuperated And I could do no wrong in the eyes of my grandfather. All he wanted was to spend time with me and all I wanted was the same. I remember playing in my backyard one summer day. My mother had gone in to make my lunch and my grandfather had stopped by and picked me up, not saying anything to my mom. Needless to say, once she called me in for lunch and I was nowhere to be found, she panicked and notified the police. Several hours later, once my grandfather and me pulled in the driveway after going out for ice cream, the police officers almost arrested him and gave him a scolding. It was funny because my grandfather couldn't understand why. I mean, it was me. I was his. How could these people tell him he couldn't be with his grandson? He just didn't get it, nor did he care to.

Most of the stories from my childhood came from different people telling them. I remember one particular story in 1979, when I was two years old. There was a very bad train derailment in Mississauga and almost the entire city was evacuated. It was terrifying for everyone that lived there. Residents had no idea what to expect or what toxic chemicals they had been exposed to as a result of the incident. The entire city was in a panic. Every street you turned down was already filled with the vehicles of others trying to escape. My parents, acting quickly, headed west into Burlington to one of my aunt's houses; my grandparents went east to Toronto to my uncle's house thinking we were close behind. But when my grandfather arrived at my uncle's house and realized I wasn't there, he made my uncle drive him back through 15 hours of traffic to pick me up. You see, he thought that if this was our last day on earth and we were going to die, then he wanted to be with me. This story gets told more often then most and I never get tired of hearing it.

Hearing all the stories of the love my grandfather had for me is very touching. And I'm telling them to you because I want to make something clear. Anxiety can hit the nicest people from the best and most loving families. Anxiety makes you feel guilty about having anxiety. It's extraordinary when you think about it but that's how anxiety works. It keeps itself hidden through all sorts of mechanisms. I know a lot of them. I've lived most of them. And the first trick that anxiety uses on people is to get them to keep quiet about it.

So you keep your anxiety to yourself. You don't want to hurt your family or friends; you don't want the shame or embarrassment for yourself or hurt those you love. So you stifle it. You might admit it once every blue moon, maybe because you can't hide it after you've had a melt down. But even then you downplay it and what it does to you. The reality is a secret only you and anxiety share.

Guilt. The first and the best of the ways to keep you half dead.

In that darkness, anxiety grows.

The last thing that anxiety wants is to have it all come out in the open and have a light shone on it. This is one of the reasons why I'm going to be really really honest about my life, all the good and all the bad. Because I've had lots of both. Maybe my anxiety wouldn't have been so crippling if I'd had only good things happen to me. But who knows. Maybe my anxiety and depression would have happened anyway. But for sure my start in life was about as good as anyone could have asked. So you can come from the nicest of families and still be a slave to anxiety.

One thing about my granddad was that he was an avid card player and would hang out at the local Italian social clubs for hours on end playing cards with all of his friends. This was his place to unwind and forget the world, and this is also where I met some of the most prominent and powerful men of the underworld in Canada. Some might say that it's no place for a child but I learned a lot in those places. I learned respect. I learned loyalty. Most importantly, it was the first place I learned fear.

Many of these men lived in fear. It was a different type of fear, I later realized. The fear these men were going through was brought upon them by themselves. It wasn't until later on in my life when I was able to actually read the newspaper that I could see just how powerful and influential these men really were. By then, I was also able to understand why they lived in such fear and how they brought that upon themselves.

When I think about it now, what bothers me most is that these men chose their lives. They chose fear. They chose fear when they had options about how they could respond to their situations which didn't include fear. I had no choice. Fear came to me. Fear found me. I know that life's unfair but this still really just pisses me off.

I know my Nonno had his own demons with fear. I never got too many details of his story. I only heard it once and once only. When he was a child himself living in Italy, his mother was a maid and he would tag along with her to help clean houses. She was cleaning a house for this particular man, who was very well connected in Italy's underworld, when another man whom he'd framed for something criminal, came through the door looking for him. Well, my great-grandmother lied and said she didn't know where he was. When the uninvited guest went around the back and found her boss, he was furious she'd lied. So after killing her boss, he went back into the house and killed my great-grandmother in front of my Nonno.

That has to change a child. Death changes people and murder doubly so. I cannot imagine what it must have done to my Nonno or how he overcame it.

I think about him still. I think about what he overcame, the quiet courage to be an immigrant and create a new life in Canada, and the love he was able to share. I got lucky. Not just because I was born into this family (although that's hugely lucky) but also because I have this role model to follow. Having someone like my grandfather gave me a fall-back, a buffer. With him, I was able to be myself. I felt safe. Anxiety ripped me apart until I felt like I was two people but with my Nonno, I could relax and be. That feeling of being, of being whole and being one, is what I strive for. Know that that feeling existed, knowing that that state of being existed was the route of out of the darkness and into the light.

EXERCISE

WRITE THE NAME OF A PERSON OR PERSONS WHO REALLY LOVE YOU AND BELIEVE IN YOU NO MATTER WHAT. DESCRIBE HOW IT FEELS TO BE WITH THAT PERSON.

_____
_____
_____
_____
_____
_____
_____
_____
_____
_____
_____
_____
_____
_____
_____
_____
_____
_____

I had it all growing up as a child except one thing – a childhood. You see, that was taken from me at the hands of those who were molesting me throughout it. My first experience of this came at the age of five. It was a family gathering and I was in the basement of my uncle and aunt's house playing with my cousin, who was years older than me, when a relative came into the room and introduced a new game. He would make my cousin touch my private parts. This "game" would continue for almost my entire childhood, getting worse as I matured.

I wish I could say it was just my uncle. But when I was around seven, my babysitter would make me massage her and touch her in places below her pants and under her top. Then she would do the same to me. Another time this happened was when my parents owned a pizzeria and next door was a Mac's Milk convenience store. The older man working there would have me pee in a cup and watch and give me candy for doing it. When I was 10 years old playing at my best friend's house, his older sister, who was around 16 at the time, decided to play hide and seek with us. She decided to hide with me, take off my pants and hers and jump on me. And that was how I lost my virginity.

Although I didn't say anything to anyone, a part of me felt this was how things are; this is life. I didn't question it.

I didn't think of it. It was my normal.

It's been really hard to unpack all this. I was well into my adulthood before I began to understand what had happened and what to make of it. At first, being molested was very confusing. They were trusted adults, people who were "good". And it was incredibly difficult because one of them was a family member. Family was everything. I think one of the reasons why I never said anything was because in a way I felt sorry for the people who were doing that to me. I was protecting "good" people from the destruction if anyone ever found out.

In a sick way, though, it also felt almost comforting, almost like a security blanket. Being molested meant that life really was as rotten as my inside was telling me that it was. It made my stress and anxiety seem like a perfectly reasonable response to the reality that the world was a dangerous place, and that if something could go wrong, then it inevitably would. So bizarrely, and this is hard to get, but being molested went from something that I couldn't understand to something I found comforting.

It's hard to write about and tell people about it because it's such a mish-mash in my head. I was a kid so things weren't that clear to begin with. In my heart of hearts, I knew it was wrong. But I had to convince myself that it was normal, and that it would all be okay and to just get through it. I told myself that I was bi-sexual so at some level, I wanted it, I liked it. In reality, I was and still am heterosexual, but I told myself that I was bi-sexual to create in my mind that it was normal to just get through it. And obviously I wasn't asking for it. I had no choice.

It made me grow up faster than I should have. I felt I had to hide it and be "normal" so that no one would know.

Lying and hiding and pretending do that. It makes kids age super fast. It's tough growing up and being at school and trying to hide what was happening to me in my personal life.

As I got older I started watching sex scenes in movies. It was insanely uncomfortable for me to see them. Every other boy my age was into this stuff, watching whatever they could whenever they could. But the sex scenes felt wrong but it was wrong because the sex scenes were right and what I was experiencing wasn't. It was almost like I was trying to convince myself that all those sex scenes in the movies that every other kid was enjoying were wrong. It made me so uncomfortable to watch them that I actually didn't. I must have been the only heterosexual teenage boy not getting off on pictures meant for heterosexual teenage boys.

EXERCISE

***STATE** ONE THING THAT IS SO CONFUSING FOR YOU THAT IT'S HARD TO KNOW WHETHER IT'S GOOD OR BAD, RIGHT OR WRONG. KNOW IT. SAY HELLO TO IT. ACKNOWLEDGE IT. ADMIT THAT IT MIGHT NOT BE CONFUSING FOR ANYONE ELSE, AND THAT LAW MIGHT BE PRETTY CLEAR ABOUT WHETHER IT'S RIGHT OR WRONG. BUT JUST LIVE FOR A MOMENT WITH THE FACT THAT IT'S CONFUSING FOR YOU. LATER, YOU CAN SORT IT ALL OUT. BUT FOR NOW, ACCEPT YOUR CONFUSION AS A STARTING POINT.*

_____
_____
_____
_____
_____
_____

I

So on the surface, I was a very happy little boy. I had the perfect life. But deep inside, I was holding on to something – fear. It controlled me and it had ever since the tender age of five when I can still vividly remember having my first anxiety attack.

It was mid May 1983 about 9:30 at night. I was just sitting in the living room and it was time for bed. I had this strong feeling of impending doom. It was hard to try and explain it to my parents because I had no idea what was going on myself, but the more I tried to explain, the worse it got for all of us. I totally grasped that my young parents could not understand and felt helpless. Can you imagine at that age I was able to comprehend that and yet all I could do was cry and panic, not being able to understand it or even being able to explain it? It made me feel isolated; I felt like I was different.

At the time, I had no idea what was going on or what it was. Could it have been from being molested? This fear wasn't the same fear that the older men at the social club were experiencing; it wasn't even the type of fear I knew from being scared of the dark.

So I did the best thing I knew how to do. I kept it quiet and tried to live a normal life. Well, nothing was normal about living life like that because you don't realize how much fear really controls your every day existence and how it makes you think. It's not just about being scared; it's about how every action, every decision, every thought you make is based on the fear you hold within yourself. It plays a huge part of who you are and it brings out the worst in you.

I became to be a troubled student. During elementary school, I was suspended more times than I can count. Although I was a very smart, my grades showed, in fact, quite the opposite. The teachers always told my parents that I got away with more than I should have because all I'd have to do is bat my baby blues at them. In grade five, they tested me for learning difficulties because they could see that there was this gap between what I could do and what my marks said I was doing. But the test showed that I was operating at a really high level. So the teachers concluded, entirely correctly, that my underperforming was a behavior crisis.

And it's true, my behavior was awful. I rebelled against every type of authority: teachers, principals, counselors. I didn't trust any of them. I think I was so difficult because I felt so alone. I thought that no one would believe me. And partly it was because of the anxiety. I was battling that one alone too. So how could someone help me when they didn't understand what I was going through. And they couldn't understand because I didn't understand and so I couldn't tell them.

So I acted out. Even though I was a troubled student, I was pretty popular because I also made a point of helping other classmates. I beat up the bullies. If a student wasn't popular or was different, I would try to make them feel like they were part of the "cool kids".

No matter how nice I make myself sound, I was still a problem. I hung around the bad kids, all the while knowing that this wasn't me. I knew I was a good person; I knew I didn't want to act that way. I knew there was more to me and how I was feeling, and it was all because of fear. I just didn't get it then and it was too overwhelming for me as a child to even try to understand it. So life continued and the fear grew and so did the molestation.

The anxiety attacks happened mainly at night. So from the moment that I woke up in the morning, I would fear going to bed at night. Imagine your very soul being put to death every night when it was time to go to sleep. That's what it's like to live daily with the fear that I kept inside. The attacks were so bad that I would vomit at around 11pm. I would stare at the clock every night and I knew that if it passed midnight and I hadn't vomited, then everything would be okay and I'd made it through.

I know now that anxiety started because I felt that I was not able to open up about what was happening to me. I suppressed my thoughts, and that led to a vicious cycle of not being able to say or act on how I felt. So what I did do was teach myself as much as possible. I pushed myself to read and learn as much as I could about what this was and how the mind worked. When I put my mind to it, I could excel in learning. One of the side effects though was that I found myself outside myself, letting things happen, allowing them, and then observing why it happened, how it affected myself and my life, and what I could do to change it. I became a scientist about myself. So at one level, learning was really useful and I have drawn on it throughout my life and I encourage everyone to learn. But at another level, I put knowledge between me and myself.

In the summer of 1985 when I was eight years old, I was spending the night at my cousin's house. At that time, he was doing extra work in movies and he'd been called to be in a film the next day. I eagerly joined and had my first experience of life on a set as an actor, and I loved it. I remember going home and begging my mother to get me into acting and, of course, with her full support, she did. Acting became my life. When I was acting, I was able to be a different person. I was able to escape the reality of my own life. I was able to become vulnerable and more open and more in touch with my feelings. It became addictive.

At this point in my life, my parents decided to move to a little town in Ontario called Burlington. The thought of being so far away from my grandfather crippled me. But there were also mixed emotions; I desperately needed a change. I was excited to start a new journey in a new place, a place that I thought I could start over and leave behind all of the horrible memories I'd kept inside me. The only person I knew in Burlington at that time was my cousin, and he welcomed me with open arms. Some of the greatest memories I have are of Burlington.

We would go on bike rides and explore the city. We spent countless hours hanging at the local arcade and just did what normal kids do. Things started to seem a little different for me; I was actually enjoying my time. I was enjoying being a kid. My grades started to improve; my life starting to improve. I was happy. It was almost like I felt this is what normal was.

In the spring of 1991, I landed a very large role in a major motion picture with some of Hollywood's biggest stars at the time. I had spent a couple of months on set with very long hours. I had no time to see my friends or really have any time to myself. Nonetheless, it was my life. Acting was me. It was something I never would've given up for anything the world, or at least that's what I thought at that time.

Then I gave it up.

I was home for the first weekend in a long time and a friend of mine had just received his license and wanted to take his mom's car out for a joyride. So a bunch of us teens met at the high school around the corner from my house. We were all just enjoying the summer night talking, laughing, and telling stories like teenagers do. I left to go home for dinner, and it was arranged that I'd meet up with them later on that night to go for a joy ride. But when I went back with another friend of mine, they never showed up. Needless to say, I was upset and angry. I couldn't figure out why my friends wouldn't have come back to pick me up. It wasn't until the next day that the sister of one of the friends I'd been with the night before, came to my house and told me the news, news that took my breath away.

She told me my friends had gone driving on a road called Number 1 Side Rd. I knew this road. We called it a roller coaster road because of the hills. We'd been there many times, speeding up and down. It made for an enjoyable time. This time, my friend had lost control of the car and he flipped it into a ditch, killing my four friends in the back.

We learned that two of our friends had survived the accident, so we quickly rushed over the hospital to see one of them. When we got there, he could barely talk he was so upset. He told us the last thing he remembered was hitting the side of the road, the driver losing control, and then ending up in a ditch. He said he managed to get out of the car and pull out the driver, causing much damage to the side of his face. He could hear two of our friends in the back screaming in agony. The car then caught on fire and he desperately tried to put it out. Neighbours came out after hearing the screaming and also tried to help but were unable to do so.

Four of my friends died that night. It was the start of another life-changing event that directed me one step closer to my death.

Burlington was a tiny and quiet town. It was the type of town where everyone knew each other. So when news of the accident got out, the entire town came together as one. It was a tragic loss, not only for the families but also for so many friends and the residents of Burlington. We all mourned together. I took it hard, not just because I lost four friends but also because I'd been so close to being in the vehicle that night.

We all quickly met together at the site of the accident and just cried, talked, and told stories. Once again, it was the usual things teenagers do. But this time, it was different. We weren't talking about funny stories that happened on the weekend or things we wanted to do later that night. We talked about death and loss. We couldn't understand how four friends could be gone just like that, in the blink of an eye. None of us had gone through or experienced a tragic event like this, and it wasn't like you could escape it because it was on every news station, every radio station, and in almost every newspaper across Ontario.

The following week, it got even worse. The residents of Burlington had to have four funerals for four teenagers. Although it was a tragic time for so many of us, it felt warm to have an entire town come together and support each other. It was June 14, 1991.

After the funeral of one our friends, a bunch of teens got together to celebrate the lives of our four friends at a place called "The Rock." It was just a little secluded area of the woods right beside Upper Middle Road. People drank, smoked the occasional joint, and just all came together to appreciate life and friendship, and to remember those we just had freshly said goodbye to and laid to rest. I was always a popular kid, very outgoing. I knew everyone. So that night, I was all over the place talking to everyone and just trying my hardest to be a teenager.

As the night turned into early morning, the crowd started to die down. I had said goodbye to a couple of friends and slowly started walking to the plaza to the Mac's Milk payphone so I could phone my father to come pick me up. As I was walking up, I could see a young woman, really just a girl still, already on the payphone. I didn't really know her well but we knew each other well enough by name and we started talking. Leslie told me that she'd broken her curfew. And she'd done this so many times before that she was now locked out of her house because her mother was getting tired of her not following the rules. She had nowhere to go. So she'd just hung up the phone with one of her friends in hopes that she was able to stay there but wasn't able to.

In all honesty, I continued to talk to Leslie because I thought she was cute. After talking about the accident and our friends who had passed away, we decided to walk to her house once again and see if maybe we could get her into her house somehow. This obviously was just an excuse so I could spend more time with her. After getting to her house and realizing that there was no way we were going to get in, we decided to head back to the plaza.

While we were there, a man approached us and began small talk. He was much taller than us, with blonde hair and blue eyes, very clean looking. Right away, I suspected him to be an undercover cop. After he'd introduced himself and asked what we were doing there, he offered us drugs and alcohol. I graciously declined and I decided to call my father to pick me up. My friend said she was going to stay and walk back home to continue knocking on the door until her mother decided to open it. I said goodbye and proceeded to walk to the street where my father was going to be waiting.

I went home with Leslie still on my mind, upset I didn't get her phone number. But I knew I'd see her again. It wasn't until later that week that we found out she'd gone missing. So I went to the police station and told them exactly what I had seen.

It was a grueling time for me. I was very confused, still hurt over the loss of my friends and now somebody I knew was missing. I remember thinking to myself, what else can happen? That's anxiety. Bad things happen and anxiety starts preparing you for the next bad thing. I couldn't focus on grieving for my friends or on my acting or Leslie because really what I'm doing is bracing myself for the next body blow. And then it came.

A couple of men, father and son I believe, were out enjoying a beautiful day fishing on Lake Gibson and they noticed pieces of concrete with what appeared to be human remains inside. What happened next was horrific. It was the infamous Paul Bernardo who had kidnapped my friend, Leslie. After they finally caught him several years later, I saw his photo in the newspapers, and I knew that this was the man I'd seen that night with her. He and his wife at the time, Karla, had brutally raped her, tortured her, chopped her up and encased her remains in cement and threw them in the lake. His face will forever be etched into my mind.

When something like that happens, you can't help but feel guilty. It's that constant voice in your head saying what if, what if I had just stayed? What if I had offered her to come sleep at my house? What if I just tried to break into her house for her to get inside? I can only imagine what her poor mother feels like. I'm positive Leslie's mother did this because in her mind she was helping Leslie become more responsible. From what I understood, Leslie's mother was a wonderful mother and an amazing woman, but I share her guilt. I kept quiet about this for a very long time because the pain was overwhelming. The guilt ate at me every single day.

It was impossible to grieve for my four dead friends. It was impossible even to grieve for Leslie. All I felt was this pain of guilt. What if... what if... if only I had done this or that... if only I'd done this then I could have done that, and really I should have, I really should have. The guilt.

After Paul Bernardo was arrested, that's when things got more real. I was interviewed numerous times by police and at one point by a detective from the FBI. I took lie detector tests and my name was published in a book. I had to go through interview after interview. Here I was, 13 years old, having just lost four friends in a car accident and was the last friend Leslie saw before being kidnapped, raped, chopped up, put in cement and thrown in the lake. It was like my acting life was meshing with my real life. Was

I in a movie or was this really happening? Does this stuff exist in the real world? Either way, I couldn't act anymore. I couldn't do much of anything anymore. I became bad again, a troubled son, a troubled student, a troubled soul with zero remorse for my existence. I had no idea what to do with myself anymore.

My parents decided it was time for change once again. So they settled in Oakville, Ontario. Moving to Oakville wasn't so bad. I had my older cousins there and immediately made friends. Not only that, I was a lot closer to my Nonno. But the reminders of the tragedies that occurred in Burlington were still fresh in my mind. Starting at a new high school, I will admit, was good because I had older cousins who also went to the same high school. This, in turn, made me very popular. All my friends were older, much older, and there was one particular person that I was introduced to – Frank. The day we met we instantly bonded like brothers. During those years, we all did so much together. Frank and I spent a lot of time together. Frank lived right around the corner from me and we were almost inseparable.

One long weekend two years later, my family had planned to go to Wasaga Beach. I remember Frank being upset because he wanted to come with us but he knew he had to go and help his parents for the busy weekend that lay ahead. Frank's parents owned a little roadside rest stop in a town called Marathon, which was over 10 hours from us. The last time I saw Frank, we were all hanging around the plaza up the street from my house, teasing him about how much fun we were going to have at Wasaga Beach that weekend without him while he was stuck working. It was all in fun and he knew that. It was probably around

8 or 9 o'clock that Thursday night. Frank got into the car, said goodbye and I'll see you soon.

I remember we decided to come back from the beach early on the Sunday because it was a little cold. Then my mother called and told me I needed to come home. I knew something was wrong. A good friend, Peter, the same friend who'd first introduced me to Frank, picked me up and brought me to my house. On the way, which was a five minute drive, Peter gave me news that made that drive seem like an eternity.

Frank had left his parent's restaurant and was walking down a dark road when a group of guys on their way to go fishing decided to pass another vehicle. Instead of passing on the opposite side of traffic, they decided to pass on the shoulder and didn't see Frank.

Yet again, I had to bury a friend. It was an awful time for all of us. It was hard, unbelievably hard, harder than I can tell. But in a sad way, I was also used to it. I was fifteen and burials of my friends had also become my normal.

I don't think that I ever really learned how to grieve for all my friends' deaths. I still hadn't processed the murder of Leslie. During these two years there was wall-to-wall coverage of the trial of Paul Bernardo with every despicable detail. I could only pretend to not hear it. But I heard it. And I couldn't dissociate Leslie from the loss of my four friends because I'd last seen her at their wake. And my good buddy, Frank. It was an awful mixture of inexpressible grief and guilt then never got let out.

EXERCISE

NAME SOMEONE(S)

YOU'VE LOST. LIST ALL THE WAYS THAT YOU GRIEVED. WHAT EXACTLY DID YOU DO? WHAT DID YOU SAY? HOW DID YOU HANDLE IT? WHAT WAS THE RESULT? WAS IT ENOUGH? ARE YOU AT PEACE WITH THAT LOSS?

_____
_____
_____
_____
_____
_____
_____
_____
_____
_____
_____
_____
_____

I

Once again, the fear came back. And this time with a vengeance.

One thing I can say in my defense is that I always stayed away from drugs and alcohol but I was bad in other ways. I fought a lot. I was never a bully though. In fact, I was the one who would beat up the bullies. It was weird, right? Here I was, fighting a lot, sleeping around with all the girls, causing trouble anywhere I could but I still had morals and values. Sort of.

The first taste of real trouble came not long after. A friend's older sister was babysitting and came across a briefcase that contained a lot of cash in it. So a group of us decided to break into the house and steal it. There were about four of us and we all split the money, which was probably over $20,000 in cash. One of the first things I did was buy a car from another friend. Can you imagine, fifteen years old, no license, driving around in a car? Yep, that was me. Obviously we all got caught and I ended up going to juvenile jail for it.

When I was in jail, my guidance counselor from high school, Fernando Costa, would come and visit me every single day and make sure I was okay. I know my parents loved and cared for me, but this was different. This was a man who believed in me. This was a man who wanted to help me and was almost a stranger at the time and I never knew why. How could this man be so selfless to want to help me? I didn't understand it at that time but I owe a lot to Fernando although I showed it differently. After I got out of detention, I continued on for those teen years being rebellious, being a shit disturber as most people would've called me, and really doing above and beyond what the normal teenagers at my age were doing. It's thanks to Fernando (who has given me permission to use his name in this book) that I later got into college. Although I never opened to him about my anxiety until later years, he was the only person in school who believed in me, and he would go above and beyond to push to my full potential.

Because of my vomiting every night as a child, I developed a condition called emetophobia. This is when you get so freaked about vomiting that it becomes an overwhelming anxiety. So you don't see a delicious meal that your mom has made for you. You see food poisoning. I never ate chicken because of fears of salmonella. All my food had to be burnt to a crisp. I stayed away from people who were sick with the common cold or who were sick in any way in case I picked up the bug and end up vomiting. I developed a hatred for Christmas because December was the stomach bug season, and what do you in December, the time of year when everyone's sickest? You go out meeting everyone, sharing food from the same serving platter, eating food they've handled, meeting all sorts of people and kissing them on the checks. I HATED Christmas. Can you imagine? Hating the best time of the year when everyone is at their most vulnerable and it's such a beautiful thing?

Everything around me was carefully scrutinized

because of the emetophobia. My hands were cracked from washing them every thirty minutes. I would open doors with my sleeves so I didn't have to touch the handle.

The emetophobia was so bad that I remember once when I was on Facetime video chat with a cousin in Italy and she had a stomach bug. I didn't sleep for three whole days thinking it would be an epidemic.

This sounds a little bit funny. And I suppose also a little bit pathetic. In real terms what happened was that I lost a ton of weight. It also spiraled from emetophobia into agoraphobia. Phobia plus plus. There's a logic to this. Because I was so frightened of getting food poisoning, I didn't want go out in case I got sick and vomited from it. So home became the only safe place. Every place else was a challenge, like a Mount Everest. I was never able to sleep over at a friend's house because I always needed to be home.

Let me give you an example. Some friends of mine and I decided to go to Florida and the day that we were going to leave, I hid my passport and I couldn't find it. I'm would make up any excuse to get out of any situation, even starting fights with people, including my wife, just to get out of wherever we were so we could go home. Most of the time I was miserable, agitated and such a ticking time bomb that any small situation could erupt into a world war.

Distraction. Anxiety makes you crave distractions, live inside distractions, and then create distractions. The best distraction is a drama. If there wasn't one happening, I made sure it did. I became a different person. It was like I had to have a split personality as a protection against the anxiety. I lied a lot and was very manipulative because I was too embarrassed to say I did these things and why I did them. I was too embarrassed to say that I needed to have a drama to distract myself from what was happening in my own head and when there wasn't the drama, I needed to create one to feel better about myself. I was too embarrassed to tell the world about anxiety.

EXERCISE

HAVE YOU EVER CREATED A DRAMA, A DISTRACTION FROM WHAT WAS GOING ON INSIDE YOUR OWN HEAD? HOW DID YOU DO IT? HOW DID IT MAKE YOU FEEL? DID IT INVOLVE LYING? OR SUGGESTING POWERFULLY SOMETHING THAT YOU KNEW WASN'T TRUE?

ONCE YOU HAVE MADE THAT LIST, STUDY IT. CAN YOU SEE A PATTERN?

_____
_____
_____
_____
_____
_____
_____
_____
_____
_____

When I was 16 years old, a couple of friends and I walked into a dance club in Mississauga. The place was completely empty. Just before we were ready to leave, a man came and began a conversation with me. He said to me, "You seem like the type of kid that knows a lot of people." He then handed me a box of flyers and said, "Make my place busy and I'll make sure I take care of you." Boy, did I ever turn that nightclub into one of the hottest places to be in Mississauga at that time. Everyone knew me; I knew everyone. I was beyond popular. Every weekend that place was jammed, the best parties in the city. I had it all: tons of money, tons of popularity, everyone wanted to be around me.

But something was still missing and I had no idea what it was. In the later months of 1996, I wanted to find myself and figure out what it was that I wanted out of life. The only time I was ever really happy was when I was with my grandfather. I would see him every single day. Before going to the clubs on the weekend, I would always stop by and spend time with him.

One night, I came home from being out and my dad said we had to talk. He told me my grandfather was diagnosed with cancer and it didn't look like a good outcome. Even as I write these words to this page, the tears still flow; the pain feels like it was yesterday. For the next couple of months, I watched my superhero fade into nothing. The strongest man I knew was ending his journey of life and leaving me alone to face mine. I remember it like it was yesterday.

The last conversation I had with my grandfather, he was lying in his hospital bed and he grabbed my hand and turned to me and said, "Don't worry, when I die I'll send you an angel."

I laughed and said, "What?"

He then said, "I took care of you my whole life. When you're ready for her, I'll send her."

I then joked around and told him to make sure she was shorter than I was, had curly hair, blue eyes, and knew how to dance salsa. We laughed and continued to talk about other things. I went home that night and I was playing on my computer when the phone rang. It was around 1:30 in the morning and for the past week or so it was common that my grandfather could never sleep and would get upset and agitated, so the nurses would call us to come to the hospital. My mother came down as usual and said we need to go to the hospital. I knew this time was different; I felt it. I knew something was wrong. All I could do was shake.

We went to the hospital, got in the elevator and as soon as the door opened for my grandfather's floor, my uncle was standing there. I remember he had tears in his eyes and all I heard him say was, "We lost him."

That walk to his room was something I don't think I can explain. I felt like I was in slow motion but everyone and everything around me was at normal speed. I could feel all the hospital staff and my family's eyes on me as I walked to his bed to say my goodbye. That night, a piece of me died and I know I'll never get it back. I don't remember much of the funeral nor do I want to. The one thing I do remember about this tragic time in my life was my father's reaction. He had just lost his father yet he was so concerned about me. I remember the next day my father took my car to get cleaned. It was just a small gesture that really meant so much to me.

My father and I never really had a relationship and I never understood why. Was it because my grandfather took on the role? Was it because my father was too young at the time and had a family to support and was always working? Or was it me? Was it my fears? Was it my anxiety? Was it the energy that I was producing that kept him away from me? I wasn't sure but to this day, it is still something that bothers me. I know my father loves me and I know him showing it is hard. He's not a bad person or a bad father. In fact, quite the opposite. He's a remarkable man with a huge heart. At the end of the day, I know he will always be there for me and love me. I think he just loves differently than my mother does.

After the passing of my Nonno, I changed. I was different; life was different. The club scene was boring me and I decided to move onto something else. I found myself going back to those Italian social clubs just so I could have a piece of my grandfather, and they welcomed me with open arms. At those places, I felt secure, I felt good. It was like my grandfather was still with me and I needed that.

Those visits, however, came with a lot more than just the comfort of the surroundings. I was in the presence of men who were not your typical men. These were men of power, men of importance, but you only read about them in books or newspapers, or saw them in the movies. It's funny because on the surface, not much went on in these places, but wow, did so much happen! There were tons of meetings, plenty of gambling, and more money going through these places than your average bank on the corner. After many years of practice, hours and hours first with my Nonno and later with other men, I became super skilled with cards, occasionally even a card shark. I also ran envelopes across the city, knowing neither what was in them, nor having the want to know; I just knew I was making money doing it.

But something inside me still wasn't satisfied.

It was around this time when my mother started working at Ford Motor Company. Living in Oakville, this was the place to work. Excellent pay, amazing benefits, and job security of course. It's not easy to get into this company and I was offered an opportunity so I thought, why not. I'll give it a shot.

I only lasted three months. This place wasn't for me. Repetitive work, hardly any advancement, and the worst part, time spent just staring at the clock waiting for the day to be over.

One day, I realized there had to be more to life than just this. Funnily enough, that same day I was struck by a forklift. I was talking to a coworker and I was leaning on a bin that was holding automotive parts. I guess the driver didn't see me. He smashed into the bin and threw me about 10 feet onto the line. I damaged my right shoulder and was off work for almost a year.

During this time, my grandmother became very sick. No doctor could figure out what was wrong with her. She went for test after test with no answers. As the days went on, her health declined. I knew what it was; it was a broken heart. Then she ended up in emergency and we were just waiting for the inevitable. I was outside the hospital room when my great aunt came out and told me that since I was one of the people closest to her to go in, I could go in and say something. I remember walking in. Most of the family was around her, my sister was holding her hand. And I leaned over her bed and whispered in her ear. "Everyone is here and we're all okay. Go be with Nonno. He needs you more I do." Then I said to her, "Just tell him to hurry and send me my angel." I remember her looking up at me, giving me a kiss. She had let out a tear and passed.

The funeral for her was a hard one but after that, I swore I would never walk into another funeral home in my life ever again. And for the most part, I haven't. It was a tough point in my life. Anxiety started turning into depression and I still wasn't sure what I was going to do with my future. Most of my family was very educated but I had more street smarts than book smarts. Although I could do pretty much anything handed to me, that wasn't going to open the doors for any good jobs. Hanging around those social clubs really opened my eyes up to a whole different world, not necessarily a good one but still a different way of living. That's why I ended up back there.

It's weird isn't it? There you are, hanging around certain people, certain places, but you know the universe has more for you. That's something I've felt almost my entire life. I remember seeing a man who would regularly frequent the social club. He would always have on lots of flashy jewelry, very high-end cars, and tons of money. After getting to know him, my curiosity got the best of me and

I had to find out how he was making so much money. It didn't take me long to find out that he owned a massage parlour. This wasn't your every day type of massage parlour. This was a full-service establishment. I remember thinking, if he could do it, I could do it too.

So I did.

I got a partner. We located a unit in Hamilton, Ontario and we started building. Literally. It took us about four months to construct it. During that time, we hired a bunch of girls and opened our doors. After about a year of doing quite well, I started to get to know the girls better and that's where I began to have a guilty conscience. Most of these girls were in school, down on their luck, or they'd been put into some pretty dangerous situations through no fault of their own. I realized I couldn't do that anymore either so I sold it. And back I went to square one.

So there I was, still confused and unable to sleep at night because the anxiety and racing mind would keep me up until the sun shone. Something about that light would make me feel safe enough to finally get some rest. My days consisted of sleeping until about two or three o'clock in the afternoon and then right back to the social clubs playing cards and gambling. I want to say I was trying to figure out what my next steps were but in reality, I was only using it as a distraction.

It was at these places where I had met a very powerful and influential man who befriended me. He took me under his wing. Thanks to him, people had a different respect for me. Call it fear and I must, although I have to admit that I liked it a little bit.

So fear is seductive. All this life is seductive. The money, the respect, the social clubs. I liked it. They liked it.

Who wouldn't like it.

So the men in these social clubs who lived with fear, who created fear in others, who were written up (not a good way) in the newspapers, made the choice to live like that. What I didn't know was that I had choices too. Life is full of choices. I didn't just choose my life. I was choosing how I responded to my life. *Life offered experiences. How I dealt with them, was the choice I made.*

What I also didn't know was that I had an anxiety disorder. But I did know that there was still something inside telling me that this path wasn't right. I couldn't see that I had any choice but to ignore that feeling. I mean really, what was I going to do? Go back and work in a factory? Sit up all night and let the anxiety control me? If you've never had anxiety before you'll never understand it. You'll do anything and everything in your power to stop it. This new friend offered me something to do, something very engaging, and that means he offered me something super distracting. I jumped on the chance.

Together we opened up an Italian sandwich shop in Barrie, Ontario. I didn't realize what I was getting myself into. It was a huge amount of work but a lot of fun too. Because the drive was so far that I found myself spending a lot of lonely nights there. Having anxiety and being alone with your thoughts is definitely not a good mix. Needless to say, Christmas 2003, I received a phone call from a friend who lived in Barrie and he told me what he thought was bad news. But for me it was a Christmas present. My restaurant was on fire; almost burned to the ground. Many looked at it as a tragedy but for me, it was a blessing. I got a little insurance money and, more importantly, I got out.

And back I was to the old question: what to do.

This time though, instead of hanging out at the social clubs again, we decided to open our own. I mean, why not? Why should we hang around at other people's social clubs, make other people money when we can just have our own? So a friend and I started one. We had Texas hold 'em games every Wednesday night. We had video arcade machines there for the old-timers to gamble on. We had card games of the Italian variety going on daily. We were doing well, having fun.

But deep down inside, that feeling was still there. As it grew worse, the anxiety and depression really started to take its toll on me. I was doing all kinds of illegal activities, living the life that I knew wasn't mine. I knew it wasn't me; I felt like I had nowhere to turn, nowhere to go. So I stayed where I felt comfortable, or at least convinced myself that I was.

I was starting to spend almost 24 hours a day at our social club and the depression got so bad that I wasn't able to escape it. The social club both caused and helped to offset the depression. This sounds contradictory but let me explain. Just by being there, I was able to distract the depression. At least, there was always somebody there and something always going on. I couldn't be alone so I wasn't. When I did leave, I'd visit a friend who was running another bar in the city. After the bar closed, he'd have card games. It was perfect for me. After my place had closed, and everybody left, I would have another place to go to, another distraction. He and I grew a friendship. We started hanging around more, but I was almost like a zombie.

One day while playing cards at the social club, my older cousin walked in. He was working up the street and decided to pop in for a visit. Growing up, my cousin and I were very close. Seeing him that day really made me feel different. I'd missed him; I wanted the closeness again. We started to hang out again. It was a different type of fun. We were like kids. We would go on motorcycle rides, sit up all night watching movies, literally just acting like kids again.

I still knew my life wasn't the life for me; this wasn't in the life that I wanted. It didn't matter anymore where I went or with whom I hung out. It was all the same shit. The only time I ever felt any freedom was when I was at home hanging out with my cousin, being a kid.

EXERCISE

LIST *ALL THE JOBS YOU'VE EVER DONE FROM BABYSITTING AND MOWING THE NEIGHBOUR'S LAWN UP TO THE JOB YOU HAVE RIGHT NOW. DID ANY OF THEM FEEL RIGHT? WAS THERE EVER THE NAGGING SUSPICION THAT THIS JOB WASN'T REALLY FOR YOU AND YOU SHOULD BE DOING SOMETHING ELSE? DID YOU KNOW IT AT THE TIME? IF SO, WHAT DID YOU DO ABOUT IT? WHAT DID YOU GUT SAY (NOT YOUR ANXIETY, NOT YOUR DEPRESSION, BUT DEEP INSIDE, THE REAL YOU).*

_____
_____
_____
_____
_____
_____

My friend's dad became ill. I supported my friend through his father's illness, sleeping on his couch and spending more time with him. Finally, my friend's father passed away. I did explain to him that I would not be able to go into the funeral home. I mean, how could I? It was the same funeral home that held my grandfather. But I assured him that I would be there if he needed anything at all. I understood his pain; I knew how close he'd been to his father and I could feel his pain was deep. The day of his father's viewing, I remember being downtown about 35 minutes away. Something came over me and I had to go. I can't explain it. I had no idea what it was, I just knew I needed to be there at that exact moment in time. I had to go to the funeral. I can still remember driving there. It was almost like a force was in control; I couldn't stop myself if I wanted to. Not really understanding what was going on, the confusion outweighed the painful memories I had of that place. I remember pulling in and having to wait for another vehicle that was pulling in directly beside me. After I parked, I needed a couple of moments to catch my breath. I wasn't going to try to understand why I needed to be there but I just needed to build the strength to be able to walk into that place again.

As I got out of the car, I heard the car door close of

the vehicle that parked beside me. When I looked up, I saw a vision of beauty. There in front of me stood a woman in her 20s. She was just a touch shorter than me, and had the most beautiful eyes I had ever seen. Something drew me to her. I wasn't sure what it was but I knew it was something. I remember having to give my head a shake. I mean at this point, I was in a relationship with another woman and I was about to walk into a place I vowed I would never go into again, a place that held the most horrible memories. So yeah, I gave my head a hell of a shake.

After getting my composure back, I went in to give my condolences to the family and greet some of the people that I knew. Just as I was leaving, my friend's wife turned the corner. Over the course of hanging around with my friend, I'd also become friends with his wife. She was fun. We would hang out, tell jokes and stories, and got to know each other as we made small talk. I was just about to leave when she said, "One second, I want to introduce you to my sister, Valerie." I think I was in a state of shock from being in that place because I didn't notice the same girl I encountered in the parking lot was standing right beside her and it was her sister, Valerie. We said hello. Our eyes locked and in that split-second, I knew I had to leave. I had done what I came to do and although I wanted to say I was there for my friend, I knew there was more to it. I was there to meet Valerie.

I know this sounds crazy, but I could swear that it was Nonno sending me an angel and giving me a good shove to make sure that we met. Since I'd discovered girls, I'd used sex as a distraction. I'd slept with so many women, and I was always searching for that ultimate sexual satisfaction, the way a heroin user always chases that first high but can never find it. I think I did that because of the molestation when I was younger. In any case, I was a total sex addict. I wasn't looking for a wife. I wasn't even looking for something serious. I was still in a relationship at the time, but trying to get out of it because I knew I wasn't happy. At that time, I didn't want another relationship. My life was in a downhill spiral. I was all surface; everybody saw a happy person. But the anxiety was still there.

A couple of days later, my friend's wife had invited me to the house. We were sitting in the backyard and almost immediately she brought up her sister's name. She decided to invite her sister over later that night. I was sitting by the fire and I heard the screen door open. I turned to look and it was her, Valerie. I was mesmerized. There was something about her I couldn't explain. Something drew me to her and no matter how hard I tried to fight that feeling, it grew. The night went on. We made small talk. The longer the night went, the longer our talks grew. I don't remember too much of what we talked about. I can remember staring deep into her eyes and trying to understand why this was happening. But of the many, many women I'd been with, I had never felt like this from just looking at a woman. She had to leave so I walked her to her car. I asked for her number and she declined. She told me she was dating somebody. I don't know if I pretended not to hear it or I didn't care. I just knew there was something about her, something about the way she made me feel and I wasn't gonna give up that easy.

I said that since she didn't want to give me her number, could she please call me when she got home so I knew she was safe? She agreed. I gave her my number. About an hour later, she called to say she'd got home safe.

I asked if she was calling me from her cell phone and she said yes. I read back the number to her. I don't think she realized call display was a thing of the future and I had it. She gave me a laugh, almost like she was in shock. I don't know if she thought I was a creep but I didn't care. I knew I had to speak to her some more. I said goodnight and told her I would definitely call her again whether she liked it or not. I've always been a man who gets what he wants but this was different. I didn't want her; I needed her. I just didn't understand why.

As I grew closer to Valerie, I started to become confused. I knew I didn't want to be with the girl I was dating but I knew there was something about Valerie that I needed. I remember thinking, "Where is my grandfather when I need him for advice?" People would always tell me they'd had dreams of my grandfather and it upset me because since 1997 when he died, I'd never had a dream with him in it. And now I needed him.

Instead, I called my aunt, someone I always called for guidance. She told me not to worry, that I was his life. I was the closest thing to him and when I needed him the most, not to worry, he would be there. A couple of days later, I had a dream. Me and my girlfriend at the time were walking down a sandy beach. In the distance, I could see a white villa. As we got close, I saw my grandfather sitting by the ocean on a lawn chair. I remember leaving my girlfriend and running up to him. To this day, I remember the smell and the touch of his face as he held me in the dream. He didn't move his lips but I could hear his voice. I remember feeling him say, "I'm proud of you. You are exactly where you need to be and you know exactly who you need to be with. Go be with her." I remember being upset in my dream because here I was safe, here there was safety. It was like something physical. I didn't want to leave it and I certainly didn't want to be with my girlfriend. But he gave me an almighty push as he said that, and I turned to look at my girlfriend. Only now it was Valerie. She was wearing a beautiful white gown and her long hair was blowing in the wind. I could see her piercing blue eyes looking at me. I saw her looking back at me and everything of my grandfather went into her. Would it be cliché to say she was my dream girl? When I woke up, I knew what I needed to do and who I needed to be with.

I broke up with my girlfriend and became closer to Valerie. She was a good girl who came from an amazing family. She was raised much like I was, very close to her grandparents. In fact, she had lived with them pretty much her whole life. Her parents were divorced and although she was very close to her mother, she was still daddy's little girl. Her grandfather worked with my great-grandfather and my grandfather and my uncle had received a gift at her grandparent's house from my baptism. Most of our families knew each other. I even grew up with one of her cousins; we went to the same elementary school.

I knew Valerie hated the social club more than anything she's ever hated in her life. I knew she hated my lifestyle. I knew she didn't agree with the friends I hung around with. I wanted her to come to the social club and she did but to her, it was more of a chore and I could see that it weighed on her. She knew I was up to no good and doing some very bad things. Many things I kept from her but the biggest secret I had hid from Valerie was my anxiety and depression. How did I explain it to her? How would she take it? So I decided that was one secret that was best left with me.

Getting closer to Valerie really made me feel different. Although the anxiety and depression were still there, her existence was more of a push in the right direction. It was about six months into our relationship when something shocking happened. I remember one night about six months after we started dating, we were at Valerie's house and watching some of her old home movies. One movie had the date on the bottom – November 16, 1997. It was my birthday and the year my grandfather died. It read "Valerie's confirmation." In the old home movie, Valerie had come walking out wearing her confirmation gown and her sash read "Saint Anthony."

She immediately turned to me and said she remembered that day. She had argued with her teacher because Valerie wanted to pick Saint Anthony and the teacher had argued that she needed to pick the name of a female saint. Valerie said she didn't know why she'd chosen Saint Anthony, she only knew she needed to.

Valerie and I knew we were destined to be together. That was when we realised all the coincidences and the number of times that our paths crossed. There is a reason why all this happened; there is a reason why I had to go to the funeral home that day to meet her. We were drawn to each other like magnets. It was a weird relationship. We fought hard and we loved hard. It was almost like we knew we were each other's soul mates but just didn't understand it.

When I met Valerie, something changed. She was the first person who I felt I was able to pen up to. She opened the door for me and it felt safe, like I could tell her anything. She made a safe place for me sexually without any judgment. I was able to satisfy my needs because I realized that what I was craving wasn't sex but a moment and a place and a person and feeling that was safe and secure. That was the first and most important step that I took towards a healthy sexuality.

It wasn't until April 2006 – I was still trying to figure out my life and the meaning behind it – I was at Valerie's house watching a movie and a contact called. I had to meet him to go over some things, and not the right kind of things. He was involved with a motorcycle gang in Toronto and I was going to help them start their own Texas hold 'em games in the city.

I told Valerie I had to leave to meet up with a friend and go with them for a drive. On the way there to meet them, Valerie continued to call me and begged me not to go. She said she had a bad feeling and wanted me to go back to be with her. We argued about it but in the end, she won. I went back to Valerie's house and we argued long and hard. I was trying to help her to understand my life and the stuff that I was into. This was me; this was what I knew and if she wanted to be a part of that, she would need to accept it. The argument didn't go too well. I left and went home.

The next day I found out that my contact was among seven men who walked into an ambush. All of them were murdered that night. It was the worst massacre in Canadian history.

Although I was shocked to hear the news, it's almost like I knew that Valerie knew not to let me leave that night. I cannot tell you how quickly I decided to propose. At the time, Valerie's father didn't want her with me. It's not that he didn't like me; Valerie had just gotten out of a relationship she'd been in for four years and immediately started dating me and he thought that she ought to have some single time. I knew he wasn't fond of my lifestyle either. Who would want their daughter with somebody like me? Guns, drug dealing, serious crime. He just didn't understand that was the surface; that wasn't who I really was. That was instead who I needed to be to survive. Really, it was a distraction, a distraction from my anxiety and depression.

I wanted to be powerful enough, strong enough inside myself, to share all this with Valerie. And I did, kind of. She knew. And we both knew that I had to get out of this life. I wanted to make the changes necessary to make Valerie happy. I wanted to feel as if I deserved Valerie. I knew that I didn't. But I badly wanted to. So I told her everything and I promised to change. What she didn't know about, and what I hadn't the strength to tell her, was the anxiety.

So believe it or not, I could tell her all about my criminal activities but I couldn't tell her about the anxiety that lay behind it all. The shame and the embarrassment kept me silent.

When I decided I was going to propose, the first person I spoke to was Valerie's older brother. Valerie respected her brother. He was like her mentor and I knew she valued his opinion more than anyone else. I figured it would be important to Valerie not only to get permission from her father, but also to get it from her brother.

Is it wrong to say I was shocked when her brother accepted and was quite happy? It filled my heart to know he approved of the proposal. Valerie's brother was a university graduate, very responsible, very well-liked. He had a long-standing job that he was very successful in, almost the exact opposite of me. After he was okay with it, we went into the house. Now was the next step: getting permission from her father. We walked in. Her brother had asked his dad to come to sit at the table and his grandfather joined. They pulled out the wine and asked if I would like a glass. I declined and as fast as I could say no, Valerie's brother said you might need a glass. We both laughed. I knew precisely what he meant. I was nervous and I don't get nervous much, so many thoughts were running through my mind.

I knew my lifestyle wasn't right for his daughter and I also knew how much love this man had for Valerie. Much like I was the golden child in my family, she was his golden child.

I asked for his permission that night and he accepted. Valerie's brother was living in Calgary at the time and I knew he wasn't going to be in Toronto for much longer. I also knew how important it was for Valerie to have him here for the proposal so I quickly started to plan.

I hired a limo and took Valerie out to a friend's restaurant. He had the entire top floor reserved just for us. After dinner, the limo took us to a place on Lakeshore called The Sunnyside Pavilion, a beautiful white building that overlooks the lake. It's funny because until I started writing this book, I didn't realize it was much like the villa I saw in my dream with my Nonno. A friend of mine owned this building and he knew I was taking Valerie there to propose. When we got there, the gate opened and we walked in. In the distance by the window was a single table with a bouquet and two chairs. We sat and started talking. I can honestly say I have never been so nervous in my life. I proposed overlooking Lake Ontario, looking into the eyes of the most beautiful woman I have ever seen in my life. Valerie said yes and I was overwhelmed with joy.

We left the building and we had the limo take us back to the social club where my car was. She wanted to go and tell our parents the good news and then go out and celebrate together. I didn't think about it until later but thank God she said yes because I had a surprise party for her at my social club. I knew it was easy to hide vehicles for the party and that my parents would be there after I proposed. So it was a good excuse to get her there. When she walked in, she was amazed that all of our family and her closest friends were there. We had a great night.

I was still hanging around my cousin at this time. He had called me late one night, knowing I'm a night owl, and asked if I wanted to come with him to work. He said he'd be at my place in about half an hour to pick me up. Sure enough, he soon showed up in a big, dirty, disgusting tanker truck. I had no idea what I was getting myself into. My cousin explained that his friend owned the company and that they collected waste fryer oil from restaurants and sold it to biofuel companies. He said it was the future, recycling this oil into biofuel and it was good for the environment. All I could think about was how dirty this truck was. Having said it, that night wasn't like work. We had a blast as we always did when we were together.

EXERCISE

***MAKE A LIST** OF ALL THOSE PEOPLE WHO ARE A GIFT IN YOUR LIFE, WHO MAKE YOU FEEL BETTER ABOUT BEING ALIVE. MAKE A LITTLE PRAYER OF THANKS FOR THEM. SCRATCH THAT. MAKE A BIG PRAYER OF THANKS.*

_____
_____
_____
_____
_____
_____
_____
_____
_____
_____
_____
_____
_____
_____

The next couple weeks, I had a lot on my mind. What was I going to do with my life? What was in store for me in the future? And most importantly, how was I going to support my future wife? During this time, I started to realize that the people who I had surrounded myself with were not for me. Continually having to watch over your shoulder or not being able to trust anyone was taking its toll. I found myself looking for an out.

I was always on edge. And not just because it was scary knowing that the same people I was involved with, the people I spent every day with and who I considered friends, could take my life for wanting out. It was that, for sure. And it would be for anybody. But it was also the anxiety. With anxiety, you're trying to control everything and everyone around you. Things need to go the way you envisioned them in your mind, the "safe" way, because if anything impeded that, then anxiety would kick in. ***Anxiety makes us look for things that haven't happened and worry about things that aren't there.*** I didn't know this.

I felt very alone and not sure who to turn to yet I was also very outgoing and social. But that was because I needed to escape the realms of daily anxiety that weighed on me like a ton of bricks. But I couldn't live this life with

Valerie, and more importantly, I didn't want to live this life. So this was a decision that didn't come easy but I felt I had no choice.

So I called a meeting with the man that brought me into this world and also the man who could take me out of it – either by death or by allowing me to go. I wasn't sure how he was going to take it. I was hoping it would go over smoothly but then again, most things up to this point in my life hadn't. I met with him and explained I couldn't go on anymore. It wasn't a life for me. The anxiety and depression were still weighing heavily on me. I wasn't able to make the decisions that I needed to make to survive in his (and by extension my) world.

He didn't take it well. After I left, looking over my shoulder became a daily routine. I continued to have card games at the club and during the off nights, went with my cousin to collected oil. I didn't look at going on with my cousin as work. It was more of a break being away from everybody and everything. But I double-checked my back. I would have been a fool not to have.

It was 2007, in the afternoon sometime. I was at a café with some friends and my father, when I received a phone call from a man I knew who was a detective with the organized crime unit. He asked where I was and said he needed to talk to me right away. I told him I would meet at a local coffee shop up the street. I was immediately worried. I figured the only time a detective would want to talk to me was either to arrest me or protect me from somebody else wanting to hurt me. I wasn't sure what I was more scared of or what I was I going to do when I heard the news he wanted to tell me.

I remember leaving the café with a friend of mine.

I was going to drop him off at home and go to meet the detective just around the corner from the café. I was stopped at a red light when a vehicle pulled in front of me and blocked me off. Before I could even react, I saw about another 20 police vehicles all with police officers pointing their guns at me.

It was a bust, but for what? They brought me into the station and arrested me for running a gambling house. Later, I found out they had also raided the cafe and confiscated all our belongings. Although I was stressed by the criminal charges I now had to face, I was relieved there weren't any threats on my life. Indeed I got stress because of a court date.

Valerie and I had booked to be married in July of 2008 – if these charges didn't find me serving jail time. Deciding what to do with my life still was distracting me daily. Having more charges to have to worry about just added to the daily stress. I still was trying to clean up my life and free myself from the guilt of how I was living for so many years, but that proved difficult.

My cousin's boss offered me a job going out in the truck and collecting oil. It was almost perfect timing and a sign to move forward with it and start something new. I must admit I was excited to start a new chapter in my life and get as far away as possible from the life I was living and the person I was pretending to be. So many thoughts were going through my mind on the first drive to my new job. It was a massive life change. I was going to be a working man and have regular hours and have to live my time at work controlled by a punch clock. For some reason it was scary!

The months passed quickly and work didn't bother

me as much as I thought it would. Plus, the judge gave me little more than a fine for breaking the law. So that was also a big relief. The anxiety and stress actually took a back seat for a while. Maybe it was because I was preoccupied planning our wedding or maybe I just figured I had no choice at that point and needed it to work. It was around March 2008 and July was just around the corner. I now know that actually something more profound was happening. *I was able to acknowledge life and accept it. Once that happens, then I could move on and start to live it. Acceptance. Fear and anxiety can't operate with acceptance.*

We had been working on our guest list for the wedding at Valerie's house when I received a phone call from my mother's friend to come to our social club because she needed to speak to me. When I arrived, my mother, father, sister and mother's friend were all there. I immediately knew something was wrong. My mother took one look at me and burst into tears. She was trying to talk but was so overwhelmed with emotions she couldn't get a word out. Her friend walked over to me, asked me to sit down. She sat next to me and said, "Your mother has been diagnosed with cancer."

I didn't believe it or shall I say, I didn't want to consider it. I tried to just run far away from everything. I couldn't take any more pain in my life. My head was ready to explode. My heart had been engulfed with pain and fear. My mother was the world to me. She was my rock. Since my grandfather died, she was the one person in my life who always stood behind me and believed in me. No matter how wrong I was, she knew the real me and I couldn't bear to think she would be taken from me. Not yet, not now. My life was just starting to change for the better. I was working hard. I was getting married. And I needed my mother behind me.

It took about a week before I was really able to even say a word and all I asked was to speak with her oncologist. My mother had given me the number and I made the call. Not the news I wanted to hear - stage 4 cancer and she needed treatment ASAP. I told the doctor that I was going to cancel the wedding and concentrate on my mom and she replied, "Anthony, if you cancel this wedding, you will kill your mother." She told me the best thing was to continue forward and allow my mother to have that as a distraction and something to look forward to. It was going to be years of chemo and treatment and we needed my mother as happy and stress free as can be.

I felt guilty. How could I be getting ready to celebrate the best day of my life while not only watching my mother suffer, but more so, having that thought in the back of my mind. We might even lose her. I did my best to enjoy the next couple of months leading up to the wedding. My mind was in a state of constant anxiety. There wasn't a day that passed that I didn't feel sick to my stomach. The guest list we'd been working on was what we sent out and many people were missing off it. But I was in no state to even deal with that.

My mother's chemo treatments started almost right away and its side effects did as well. She was fragile, had lost all her hair and you could see the pain in her eyes but she pushed forward and on the surface, acted like everything was normal, something I was very familiar with – dying on the inside and pretending on the outside.

I did as much as I could to get my mother involved

in the planning. As sick as she was, she completed all the centerpieces for the tables and insisted on doing all the flowers. I couldn't believe it. In her state, she was so strong to be able to perform such a task and did she ever! Everything turned out better than I could have ever imagined. My mother's floral expertise really showed and it was starting to all come together. The two weeks before the wedding were almost like a vacation from my stresses and anxiety. Everything was planned. There was little left to do. I had some of my relatives from Italy fly in for the wedding and we made the best of those two weeks. Knowing my mother was surrounded by people she loved the most and was able to enjoy herself as best as she could comforted me. But I still knew she was suffering on the inside from the chemotherapy and that killed me just as much as it made her feel.

On July 12, 2008, my wedding day, I woke up that morning wondering if I was making the right decision, I had lived a life of someone that I wasn't for so long, being controlled by anxiety. How was I able to take vows with the most amazing woman I have ever met? My thought was that I could potentially destroy her life with what I was going through. I always had hope that I would be able to overcome this anxiety and I would break free from its chains but was I willing to take the chance with her? I will admit I had cold feet but not the typical type of cold feet. I knew I loved Valerie with all my heart and I needed her more than anything in my life. I just felt like she deserved better; in fact, I know she did.

In my forty-one years on this planet, that day is the one and only day I remember from when I woke up to when I fell asleep. Living with anxiety you don't remember much of anything. All day is like a survival and when you look back on the day it's like insta-snaps. You may remember the photo being taken but you have no idea what happened before or after. So your life is a collection of snapshots accidentally taken every few hours. So I could remember waking up but not going to work. I could remember leaving work but not getting home. The pictures were those rare moments when the anxiety eases a little, enough so that you can become aware of your surroundings and what's going on and you register it all in your brain. That's how anxiety robs you or your own life. You literally can't remember it because you're so focused on survival.

But not my wedding day. I remember every blessed moment.

We arrived at the church and I broke into tears. And no matter what I did, I wasn't able to stop them from streaming down my checks. It was time. I was instructed to walk with the priest to meet my parents at the top of the aisle to make that walk down to the altar. The priest had started walking and I am still in shock with the number of people that were there to witness these vows. There were at least 200 eyes staring at me. I still think they were just concerned with the amount of crying I was doing. I managed to hold myself together long enough to make it to my parents but as soon as I saw my mother, it started again. She looked beautiful, like nothing was wrong, like she wasn't sick. I could only feel happy seeing her and my father standing there so proud, ready to walk their son on the start of his journey with a new bride. I cherished every second of that walk with the cameras flashing and the videos streaming. I only had one thing on my mind:

my parents and their grace, their strength and after many years of marriage and all they'd been through, being able to present and walk their eldest and only son down the aisle to start a new chapter in his life. It was a very proud moment for us all.

As I stood at the end of the alter watching our bridal party come one by one, I had a sense of peace. I was relaxed. I remember my uncle being in front of me so I wasn't able to see the front of the aisle. There was a long pause in between our bridal party coming. Just as I was trying to grasp what was happening, the music changed and Pachelbel's Canon began to play. My uncle shifted and all I remember seeing was pure bliss.

To this day, trying to explain in detail has proven to be difficult. The sun was blaring from the open doors behind her; she was glowing like an angel. I will say this it was the MOST beautiful image I had ever seen and I cried and couldn't stop. She made her way to me and took my hand and reached in for a kiss. I think it was either not enough sleep on her end or the fact we hadn't seen each other for almost 3 days prior but I had to push her back telling her we weren't at that part of the ceremony yet. We both laughed and it was exactly what I needed to regain my composure.

The wedding was a fairytale. When Valerie and I arrived at the banquet hall after taking our pictures, we were very shocked to see a lineup of people exiting the door and around the building. We were in disbelief that this many people showed up to celebrate this day with us. I still say that all those people came because they couldn't believe me of all people was getting married and that I'd finally found a person to spend the rest of my life with. We greeted all our guests, and after almost two hours, it was party time.

I wanted to give Valerie an entrance that she deserved, an entrance that is only in books. I had rented a horse and carriage and the hall was equipped with a large rear drive in door so we could enter right into the building in our chariot. And what an entrance it was! One that's still talked about to this day. We stayed at that hall filled with people until after 4 am, until the DJ couldn't take it anymore and had to call it a night. For us, that night was more than just two people starting a new life together, it was 650 people coming together to support us and share a moment that we will forever cherish. It was and still is the best day I have had in my entire life.

The next day, we headed to Florida for our honeymoon. We were going to drive because with anxiety, getting on a plane was next to impossible. This is how anxiety shapes your life, including super important times like your honeymoon.

We headed to Orlando to a house we'd rented months before. And because there was no TV in the bedroom, I had to take the mattress out of the room and place it on the floor in the living room so we could have a TV for night-time when my anxiety would be at its highest. We spent one day at Universal Studios and obviously, it was a struggle for me to be anywhere other than the comfort of my own home and surroundings. That night I was trying my hardest to make any excuse I could to head back home. I persuaded Valerie to spend the rest of our honeymoon in Daytona Beach. In my mind, it was one step closer to heading home. Not that I wasn't happy to be there with my new bride. I just couldn't enjoy myself dealing with anxiety 24 hours a day.

We arrived in Daytona, rented a hotel and spent the day on the beach and sightseeing. I will say it was tons of fun until nighttime came. Then anxiety reminded me it was still there. That night, I couldn't take it anymore and convinced Valerie to leave and head back home. Without question, her knowing what I was going through supported the decision. Valerie never really understood anxiety, but she did take into consideration the pain I was going through.

We got home the next day and although I was happy to be there, the usual thing then happened to me: I feel ashamed, guilty and disgusted with myself for cutting our honeymoon short and depriving my wife of that experience. It was just one more to add to the massive stack of books filed in the back of my mind.

Life continued where it had left off. I was still collecting oil at night. Valerie was working at Shoppers Drug Mart, and anxiety was still present in my life. We were renting a condo in the heart of Mississauga and expecting our first child.

Life was getting real. Responsibility was being forced into my life and it was eating alive at me, not because I wasn't ready for it or I couldn't do it, but because I was controlled by anxiety and depression. And anxiety was winning the battle.

At this time at work, our boss was getting fed up with the amount of oil that was being collected and had instructed some employees to start stealing it back from the competitors who'd been taking it from us. I didn't like this. I was trying to start a better life, an honest one, a life were I didn't have to continue looking over my shoulders constantly. I mean, I had enough to have to deal with battling anxiety and depression. I didn't want any more negativity weighing me down. I decided I needed to quit imagining having a condo, while my wife was expecting a baby and I produced no income.

Valerie, the supportive wife that she was, understood and we moved into her father's basement. The next month, I secured another job with a company in the same field and sure enough, not more than 5 months into it, oil theft came back into the equation. I couldn't believe it. Here I was, trying to find security and a honest living, and all I was being given was the same life I'd been living before.

I finally said enough was enough and started my own oil collecting company. I borrowed $120,000 from an acquaintance. I started it and it took off. We rented a shop in the Mississauga area, bought a new truck and hired people and the accounts started rolling in. Business was good; things were starting to look up. I spent two years building the company from the ground up. I had a beautiful wife, a spectacular little baby boy at home and a promising future. And just like that, in one phone call, it was all taken from me.

My partner called me in for a meeting and advised me that he wanted to buy me out. Let me spell it out. He was taking over and I was out. I'm sure he figured with the amount of money we were making, and how easy I'd made it seem running the place, greed took a step in his direction. I was strong-armed out, jobless and not sure where to turn.

The emetophobia (fear of vomiting) and agoraphobia (fear of places) developed into a crisis. I mean, how could I go anywhere? What if people were sick? What if I caught something? Not to mention eating was limited because of the fear of contracting food poisoning. Those next months proved to be the worst days of my life. I was a disaster. I was weak; I dropped to 110 pounds. My mental state was all over the place. I was behaving out of the normal. It wasn't right; I wasn't good. Everything needed to be controlled. I had to make sure everything and everyone was how I wanted it to be. I would go days without sleeping and more without eating. I fought with everyone and acted like a different person altogether. I had to have a friend over at night because I couldn't stand to be alone.

I felt like a soldier always on guard, always tense and ready to strike at any moment. But there was never any danger there, except what the anxiety made me feel or believe. I was at war with invented and invisible enemies. The real me would only ever pop out occasionally and then people would see the real me, who I really was. I cherished those moments. But at this point in my life, the real me was flattened under the weight of mountains.

If you asked me now what I'd been afraid of the only answer I could give was ME. *Fear is merely the anticipation of the unknown.* Once you know what it is, then the fear will no longer exist. I was scared I wouldn't be able to say how I felt, that I'd be judged, or what I was thinking or feeling wouldn't be good enough, that it was all insufficient, that I would fail. And the failure would have been comprehensive. It was failure of a man, as a human being.

I know now that I was trapped in letting go of the old me and too scared to change because I was safe in that old me. I was scared of change and got "stuck" growing out of the old me. There's an old saying: better the devil you know than the devil you don't. I was thinking, I'm safe here in this world; I can survive and keep surviving because I've already been here so long, surviving. I got this one.

And yet, I so didn't.

While Valerie slept, I was taking at least six pills a day for anti-nausea and everything was only getting worse. Everyone could see the state I was in and the suffering I was going through but they neither understood it nor knew how to help with it. I was fighting with everyone, my family and Valerie's family included, and I just couldn't take it anymore. I didn't want to live, and moreover, I didn't want to have Valerie carry this burden anymore.

So I planned. I planned to end my life. I chose a date and purchased a gun from an associate of mine and prepared myself for that fateful night. As crazy as this sounds, it almost like during all this time I was able to have an out-of-body experience. I was able to see the anxiety and how I was acting and what it was doing to me and observe everything.

It was about five days before I had planned on doing it when Valerie's dad came home and said he'd met a lady that does energy healing and he thought I might benefit from it. When Valerie brought this to my attention, I didn't care too much to hear it. I was focused on the end of my life. I had already given up trying anything or anyone. I had already gone to see about six different psychologists, some psychotherapists, different medications, acupuncture and everything else under the sun. I was convinced nothing would work. After all of that, what could energy healing do for me, really? Like, come on. It was nothing I believed in and I didn't care too much to even want to understand it. At that point, I just wanted to die.

Valerie begged me to go and see this lady and I agreed, but not because I had hope that she could help but because I didn't want to end my life and have Valerie left behind wondering what if? What if she had pushed me to go? Had she done enough? I was not too fond of those thoughts. I mean, I was ending my life to give her a better one. So I had her make the appointment.

She set the appointment for two days later and I made my way. I got lost, and frustration grew. All my emotions were starting to surface. All the anxiety was there with a vengeance. I was cut off by a bus and I'd had enough. I pulled over and had a fight with the driver. It was awful. I was a madman. I just couldn't control myself any longer. It was my breaking point.

I pulled into a plaza and drove to the back. I parked the car and pulled out my gun. Funny enough, "Sail" by Awolnation was playing but all that was on my mind was gaining the strength to pull the trigger. I remember it was frigid out that night but I was profusely sweating. Although many thoughts were racing through my mind, the one that stood out the most was Valerie. I needed to do this for us. More importantly, for her.

I pumped myself up and said my goodbyes out loud to my mom dad, sister and Valerie. I asked for forgiveness, apologized, and pulled the trigger.

I heard a click.

I wasn't sure what happened. My breath was taken away by all the adrenaline pumping crazily through me so I wasn't breathing and felt no need to. I'd pulled the trigger but there was no pain whatsoever. Was I dead? Was that it? Was it finally all over? Then the realization I was alive, that I'd managed to screw even that up. There was a powerful regret, like being slammed with a concrete fist, that it hadn't worked. I immediately collapsed. My head pressed against my hand and the pressure pulled the trigger a second time. That time the gun did go off.

It was so loud and powerful. I remember it forcing my head to the left and all I felt was a burning feeling and then total silence and darkness.

The only reason I knew I was still alive when I came to minutes later was the ringing in my ear and the burning feeling up the side of my face. The bullet had plowed a groove along my hairline and exited the car. Being so close to the muzzle, the explosion had knocked me out. I was slightly injured, permanently scarred and completely different.

I was aware; I was present. I felt vulnerable. It was the first time in my life I was living in that exact moment.

It was almost like I was cured of my anxiety and depression. I had the secret of overcoming it. I just didn't know how to express it.

I sat there for a couple of hours just thinking about what had happened and how I felt. I was like a new man, a new person. It was so hard to try and grasp it but something came over me, and I knew this was different. I felt different. I was different.

I went straight home and I remember walking in the door and looking at Valerie and thinking, she deserves me, she deserves me to give it a fair shot. What had I been thinking of to kill myself? She'd been struggling for years dealing with my behaviour, standing behind me through all the poor decisions and all the fighting I was doing with everyone. At the end of the day, she loved me unconditionally.

That was the first night in over 20 years that I didn't need anyone to come over. I didn't need to take any medications. I lay down on the couch and just became lost in my thoughts.

The next morning, I woke up and felt different. Valerie had heard me wake up and made me a coffee as she did every morning. I went into the backyard so I could have my regular cigarette.

As I approached the yard, everything was different. I could see green on the trees. I know trees are green and that's what everyone sees but for me, it was different. I could see the green vividly. Everything looked different to me. It was all so detailed I was aware. I was present and it felt like a different world for me. *Life is amazing, once you're able to see it.*

I broke out into tears. Valerie ran over asking me what was wrong. All I could say was "nothing." As hard as I tried to explain it, I just couldn't. She was just as confused as I was. It was the first time I was relaxed. I didn't have to feel the anxiety or depression; it was surreal to me that for once nothing was wrong. I didn't know how to react, how to think or even what to do. I just knew to enjoy that moment for once in my life.

You don't realize how vulnerable you are when you're that close to killing yourself. My entire life I'd been taught that being vulnerable was a bad thing. It was something that you didn't want to be. But for me, that wasn't the case. Vulnerability has worked in my favour. I became more open; I could adapt more to my surroundings. I was listening to people and actually hearing what they had to say. Things started to become easier for me every second. I was living for that moment and it was the start of a new beginning for me. Although I was lost with everything that was going on, I'd never felt that much control before.

I wasn't sure how long it would last so I took advantage of it right away. I wanted to tap into my mind and make sense of it all. I enrolled in school and studied psychology. For the past twenty years of my life, all I'd done was read about anxiety and depression, studies of the mind, brain and anything else I could read that would either explain what was going on or how I was able to overcome it. While I was in school, I was fascinated to learn about the mind and other people's theories on it.

The more I was there, however, the more it made me not want to be there. I considered it "textbook psychology." Many of these great minds have never experienced anxiety or depression. How could they possibly help me to understand it or others to overcome it? Most of it was what medication should we prescribe and from there, it was just adding more medications or changing the dosage of the ones people were already taking. It didn't take me long to figure out I wasn't going to get my answers from a textbook. And I had more than any book; I had the first-hand experience.

I dropped out and decided I would figure this all out on my own. Life was better for me and things were starting to make sense. How and why I was acting the way I was, how fear controlled me and made me react to it and make the poor decisions I was making out of pure desperation. I was no longer desperate; I was able to comprehend everything that was happening and take things one small step at a time.

It was December, and I received a phone call from my ex-partner at the oil company. I went to meet up with him for a coffee and he explained he could no longer run the company and asked if I wanted it back. I anxiously agreed and started right away. The company grew more and more, and life started to make sense.

We now had two beautiful children at home and were in the process of purchasing our first home. I hired a friend to come in and help with the business because it had proved too big for me to handle alone. I started a foundation for kids with cancer and was actively giving back to families who were dealing with the hardship of a child affected by this. It was the least I could do. I had lost my grandfather and so many other relatives to cancer. My mother was living with it but at least we still had her, and we were all too familiar with the struggle this disease presents to families. I just wanted to do all I could to help.

The business was lucrative and the foundation was starting to come along. I was getting a rather large following of families and children with cancer pouring in from the United States. I became friends with one 13-year-old boy from just over the border. We spoke almost every night for two years. One day, I got a phone call from his mother explaining to me that his last wish was to come to Canada to meet me. I was honoured and we quickly made it happen. I was like a child at Christmas. He came to visit for a weekend. During his time here, he got really sick and we had to rush him to the hospital. The doctors had to revive him a couple of times. We were all by his side when he gained consciousness. He turned to me and said, "Anthony, don't worry about me. I don't regret getting cancer because if I never got sick, I never would've been able to meet somebody like you." There wasn't a dry eye in the room.

This little 13-year-old boy taught me so much that night. He only added encouragement in this world to help me continue my journey. He was airlifted back to his home hospital. I got a call from his mother shortly after. Death was to come any second and he asked if I could come. I did. I drove down to see him. I was able to say my final goodbyes and more importantly, thanked him for teaching me the value of life and how we should appreciate the small things that are given to us. *Live life for the moment because that may be all we have.*

I remember learning in university a theory called "savouring". It's when you can go back to moments in the past and remember them with ease, and they make you feel like they just happened. You're able to rekindle that feeling and emotion. From that theory I decided that there are two different types of people. Some wish they could go back to those times and others remember and cherish them but are looking for more in the future. The first group of people who want to go back had never present and aware in that moment in the first place. So they were not able to grasp the full potential of their emotions with that memory. But if you live fully in the moment, being aware, then you have already fully inhabited that moment in space and time. And it was a great moment. But there are more great moments in the future, which you also don't want to miss because you're living in the past. And you're living in a great moment right now, right this very second. And you don't want to miss it either.

Life continued for me and my family – and that boy always was on my mind. Everything I learned from him came out in every daily activity. I started to appreciate life more, to take the time to help myself, and get myself to where I need it to be. Everyday, life was changing for me. Ever since the day I decided to take my own life, my eyes became more and more open.

I started spending more time helping people. Valerie's cousin, Briana, was a troubled child at the tender age of fifteen, with her own quite a remarkable story to tell. But I'll leave that for her to tell you. We ended up taking in Briana as one of our own. I see a lot of me in Briana. She was depressed, driven with anxiety and cutting herself just to take away the pain. It affected her behaviour as anxiety always does. She was barely passing in school. She was very rebellious and exhibited the exact same signs I'd done. I knew I had to take action. I worked with her very closely and gave her all the knowledge I had on how I was able to overcome it. It was a rough couple of years but with time and patience, Briana has grown to not only successfully graduate, but also graduate with 3 awards and a red seal on her diploma! I couldn't have been prouder.

Just like the little boy we lost from cancer, I also learned a lot from Briana. I was able to see how I'd reacted to things when I was younger. I recognized how I interpreted things when driven with anxiety and depression. All the fighting throughout the years, all that behaviour, was a direct result of my actions. It was how I saw things, how I wanted things. It was how I needed things to be because of the fear.

It was amazing to overcome it. But the best part of it was being able to see how I was and admit the wrongs I'd done in my life. I realized that the only time the wrong existed was when I was blind to it. Once I was able to admit it, there's no such thing as wrong. I considered it learning, taking responsibility for my actions, and making it better, not only for everybody else but more importantly, for myself.

Things began to be peaceful. My children started to behave differently. My daughter had started acting just like I'd once done when I was her age and I'd missed all the warning signs. I insisted on living in the moment and being aware. My children would ask me to lie down with them at night and usually I'd be too busy and to do that. But then it struck me that if my friends who had just lost their thirteen year old son could see me, what would they say. They would have given anything to lie with him again. There is nothing so important that should take you away from spending time with your children. So I concentrated on the foundation and spent more time with my family after so many years of being blind to the important things. Once I came home from work and my eldest son came running to the door to me. That had never happened before. My marriage grew stronger and deeper. Everything in my life was perfect.

My wife encouraged me to get back involved in acting, as it was always my greatest passion. Acting had always been an escape for me. With acting, I was able to be vulnerable and show emotions and release everything that I had been holding internally. Being vulnerable doesn't mean that you are weak. *Being vulnerable means that you are brave enough not to be naïve about what it takes to live.* Acting really helped me back then, and that's why I love it so much once I became an adult. I was able to learn so much about myself and my emotions from acting.

But it had been over 20 years and I knew nobody in

that industry anymore except for one woman, the same woman who got me involved when I was just a child. Valerie encouraged me to call her, even after I insisted that there's no way she would remember me. Valerie made a bet. She said, people always remember you, you have that energy with people. I said to my wife, if she remembers me, this is a sign for me to continue my passion. I tracked down her number and phoned her on Monday. Not only did she remember me, she had me booked that following Friday on a hit show in Toronto. I was back to where I belonged. And Valerie won her bet.

While I was on set filming, I was speaking to another actor and we started sharing our stories. After hearing mine and how I was able to overcome anxiety and depression and a failed suicide attempt, he told me that it had been inspirational to hear them and that there are so many other people out there suffering in silence. He said that it would be beneficial to tell my story out loud to more people and try to help those in need.

So I did. I spoke with a close friend of mine who had a production company and asked if he would be able to put together some videos for me speaking of my anxiety and depression and how I was able to overcome it. We quickly got to work. We filmed five short videos going into full detail. We also included Valerie's take on the ordeal and how it was for her having to live with somebody with anxiety and depression. Briana also got involved and told her story.

The videos were quite successful. What was more outstanding was the number of people all over the world who contacted me asking for help. I was in a state of disbelief. All these people were coming to me for help.

Not only that, just how many people were suffering alone. I had no idea. It was heartbreaking.

I knew I needed to help these people so I concentrated all my time doing so. It wasn't until I received a phone call from my bank manager telling me my mortgage cheque bounced that I discovered we had no money in our account.

I quickly rushed over to the office and found it deserted. No employees, nobody there but a stack of bills on the desk. It didn't take me long to figure out what had happened. It was my fault. I had been paying so much attention to helping people that I'd lost touch with my company. In a way I felt like I deserved it but my family didn't. As hard as this is to sometimes admit, *everything in front of me, in front of you, in front of everyone you know and love, it's there because we all chose it to be there. You, me, and them. We make our own destiny.*

Still. The destiny I'd made for myself was uncomfortable. I had no company, no income, and we were about a month away from losing our home, a home I built with my own two hands. The sad part was I couldn't even provide food to put on the family table.

Quickly my mother and father-in-law stepped in to help. We cleaned up the house and put it up for sale. We moved back into my father-in-law's home and strangely enough, we all learned a valuable lesson.

These possessions were not significant. Money wasn't important because when you have none and you've lost everything and end up homeless, it's at that moment you realize what's essential: love, strength, and most importantly, being able to be present and aware to learn that lesson.

I firmly believe the universe does these things to us so we can learn. I always say there's no such thing as a bad day; you are just not paying attention to what that day is trying to teach you. It's funny because when I thought I had it all, money, nice cars, designer clothes, a big beautiful home, thriving company, I really didn't have anything of importance.

What was important was in me. It was the love I have for my family and the love they have for me.

We lost everything that year but we gained something that money can't buy, something that is priceless. Something most people wish for and dream of. We were able to understand and answer that number one asked question in the world: what is the meaning of life?

It's just loving life and being the best person you can be.

Everyone in our lives is here to teach us something. Once you understand that, you're able to live life to the fullest by simple being aware and present and embracing it. While you are aware you can truly see the impact you have on others.

So in ten words or less, what is it? *The meaning of life is us.*

EXERCISE

WRITE DOWN *THE NAMES OF THE TEN PEOPLE YOU'RE CLOSEST TO. WHAT HAVE YOU LEARNED FROM THEM? WHAT IMPACT HAVE YOU HAD ON THEM? WHEN YOU'RE DONE, WRITE DOWN ANOTHER TEN. RINSE AND REPEAT. RECOGNISE WHAT YOU'VE LEARNED AND WHAT YOU ARE TEACHING. IS THERE A PATTERN?*

_____
_____
_____
_____
_____
_____
_____
_____
_____
_____
_____

I

INTRODUCTION
to Part 2

Living with anxiety, your mind fails to shut off. Anxiety erases the off button. Either you're constantly worried about the future or dwelling in the past. It is having persistent inconsistent thoughts sparking every chemical in the brain. Remember those old comics where the good guys and the bad guys get into fights and the little squares are brightly filled with KAPOWs, ZAPS, THWACKs? That's my brain on anxiety.

Every day is a fight and you isolate yourself because you feel nobody will understand. So you end up living not only a life of constant struggle, but also a life of lonely struggle. One of the main thoughts of living with anxiety and depression is, "Nobody gets it, nobody will ever understand."

I'm here to tell you that you are wrong. I do understand, better than most. This is something I have lived with for over 30 years. And for me, those alienating thoughts didn't stop there. They became worse day after day until I couldn't take it anymore.

For over 30 years I was lost. Not only was I sucked into the depths of anxiety and depression but my overall health was also following down the same dark hole. Every second that passed I was plummeting deeper into the darkness. Living with this condition is like seeing the beautiful sun in the outdoors but not feeling the warmth of it on your face, until the day comes when you cannot bear the sun, and you keep your body isolated in the darkness. At the tender age of five I can still vividly remember my first introduction to anxiety, and at such a young age it proved difficult for me not only to try and understand what this horrible feeling was but also how to communicate it to those around me. There was nothing I can do, besides allow this emotion to overtake my entire existence. And by god but it did so with a vengeance. I was not living life for me, the real me, I was living life for my thoughts, and this, in turn, caused disastrous repercussions. Most of the life I was living was in fear and all the emotions associated with it.

I have been through many hardships in my short life, probably more than most people have experienced in a lifetime. A few situations had even put me staring death in the face closer then I would have liked, and on the fateful night I made the decision to put my self close to death. I was so engulfed with anxiety and depression 24 hours of the day that I knew I could not continue to live under these circumstances. When I put the gun to my head and pulled the trigger that night, I discovered a new emotion: regret.

It was regret that proved more powerful than a bullet

in my head. It set off a chemical chain reaction through my entire system that changed my life forever.

In that instant, it took me to a higher sense of awareness than 30 years of studying anxiety and the mind ever offered me. Everything came to me in that very split second. But I was not yet able to fully understand it. The best way for me to explain it, I could see clear as day directly in front of me $1+1 = 2$.

But I wasn't able to communicate it. I understood the equation and I also understood how to obtain the answer but being able to say it out loud was difficult. I'm not a wordy guy. I do things. So talking about it and explaining it, was tough. Although in my mind I knew I had embarked on a magnificent discovery, my soul was at such peace that for once in my life, for once, I just sat there and enjoyed it.

The next morning it hit me harder. I remember sitting in the backyard with my wife having our morning coffee, like we always did in the warmer months, when I turned and looked at a tree we had in the middle of our yard. I immediately burst out into tears. My loving caring wife quickly came to my side, comforting me until finally, in confusion, she asked what was wrong. I turned to her and replied, "The leaves on the tree are green." That confused her even more. You see, Valerie was all too familiar with what I was going through in my life with anxiety and depression, and although she was the best support system anyone could ever have, it was hard for her to understand how lousy living with anxiety really is.

Living in those conditions I guess the best way to explain it is, everything you see is in black-and-white. It's like your mind is so preoccupied worrying about the future and not being able to let go of the past that you are not able to process the present. And for me that changed. I knew I had the answers. I just needed to extract them from deep within my mind.

It took me ten years to finally understand these thoughts and perfect them. There are so many great minds that, like myself, have studied intensely on the subjects of anxiety, depression and the genetic structure of the mind and body. I considered these to all be "Textbook Psychology". One thing I noticed with most of these doctors and theorists was, none suffered with any of the ailments and traumas I had experienced most of my life.

Although I came out of those studies with a vast array of knowledge on neuroscience, I knew if I wanted to change – and more importantly help others – I needed to keep it simple. From my learning and my life, I was able to develop five steps. These steps require you to think things through. These steps inform you, explaining why you are experiencing what you are experiencing and suggest that with that understanding you can think about your own behavior and your thoughts and your own fears. These steps, I assure you, will guide you to a higher sense of awareness so that you will be able to live your life to the fullest.

They changed my life. They can change yours too.

STEP ONE

The key to understanding your life and all the prodigious gifts that come with it is to first understand yourself, who you are, where you are, where you want to be, and ultimately who you want to become. Like that's easy, I know. The exercises in Part 1 should have helped you to understand yourself a little better.

Personally, I find it helps if I also understand the biology behind it all. It helps a little with the self-forgiveness knowing that there is an entirely physical reason for this nasty dynamic that I got myself caught in.

The brain is such an advanced tool and consists of many functions, and one of those functions is protection. When any type of worry enters your mind, your brain will perceive that as a danger or threat. It is essential to know that this fight or flight response can be activated with both real and imaginary perceptions of danger. It doesn't matter because the brain's response will be the same. It will cause your system to begin the "fight or flight response", also known as the acute stress response. The fight or flight response was first introduced in the early 1920s by physiologist Walter Cannon. This response causes a biochemical reaction throughout the body. It releases certain hormones like adrenaline and cortisol, which speeds up the heart rate, slows digestion, shunts blood flow to major muscle groups and changes various autonomic nervous functions giving the body a burst of energy and strength. This leads to several other responses both emotionally and physically. There is no logical thinking in this state. It has only one function – to help us fight or run away from the danger that is in front of us. After the threat has passed, it usually takes up to one hour for the relaxation response to bring our levels back to normal.

During this chronic stress, the relaxation response does not happen enough and over time, stress can causes extreme damage to our bodies. The body's response to stress can cause disastrous effects on your overall health and well-being. From the top of your head to the tips of your toes, the result is undeniably severe. Make no mistake – stress is the number one killer.

Process that for a minute because it's truly bizarre. Your thoughts, something that you merely think about, can cause a reaction to ripple throughout your body that can put you in serious harm and in some cases, death.

In the same token, your mind has been known to cure you through meditation. Meditation can alter that flight-fight response.

Either way you look at it, the mind is a potent tool we all possess and when used correctly, can propel us into a life we have only dreamed of.

So how do we do it? How do we use this tool we all carry with us daily, to live a life with an abundance of health, wealth, and happiness? Simple.

The first step is to be present/be aware. Each and every day our minds are in constant thought, from the time we wake up until the time we go to sleep. From simple things like, "What am I going to wear?" "Does this outfit look good?" "What am I going to make for dinner?" or "Am I getting enough sleep?" and so on and so on, to really complex struggles like, "Is this ethical?" So much so that the thoughts become a part of us, and we become our thoughts.

Now I'm not saying to stop having thoughts. For one thing, we couldn't stop all our thoughts. We need them just to get out of bed in the morning.

The problem is that we get so consumed with our thoughts that we mistake them for something else. Anxiety and stress acting through us makes us over-think our thinking.

We need to be aware that ***we are not our thoughts.***

We're merely observers of them; our thoughts are not real until we take action on them. It's up to you to make your thoughts reality – if you choose to do so. Life is all about perspective and choice. Your perspective is your thoughts and your choice is taking the action as the result of those thoughts. Think of your thoughts as a road map with various routes and you are able to choose which route you feel is best for you. If the route you've chosen turns out not to be the best, then your perception of the situation tells you that. Then you get to choose another route: go back to the beginning, take a cut across to another road, or even create a new road altogether. Your perspective can always change once you open your mind to it. Our lives are constructed on our choices and most of the time we fail to understand we have complete control of those choices.

For example, there's nothing wrong with planning for the future. But when you're living in the future, that's when the problems occur. So we can't stop having thoughts. But we can stop our thoughts from consuming us. Once we are consumed with our thoughts, we are not present or not aware and lose touch with our reality. Plan for the future. But there's no need to live in it. It hasn't happened yet and most things you worry about or anticipate never actually happen anyway. If they do happen then they aren't as bad you thought they were going to be.

Myself, I spent all my time thinking about becoming sick. So I wasted valuable time that I was actually healthy. Irony of ironies, all that worry does actually make you sick. And once you become sick, it's horrible and I don't recommend it, but then you get better. And you see that actually being sick wasn't really that bad.

Or look at your workplace. There are many people who do not enjoy going to work every day. You might be one of them. Try looking at it from a different perspective. Is it the work you don't like? Is it the environment? Is it your co-workers? What can you do to change these things? Or even, is it you?

The critical thing to understand about life is that *no matter what, we always have a choice* in every situation. That could mean you could change things merely by changing your perspective on things. By living in the moment and not having to worry about the future you instead know that whatever occurs, you will handle it as it comes – to the best of your abilities. By having a clear mind and the strength that stress has not taken from you, the road map can help you to enjoy the moment and make better, more logical decisions for you in that time.

But it's hard to know how to live in the present when you are consumed with anxiety and stress. So let's take this whole thing apart, this living in the moment, and really examine it.

They say there are two things that are guaranteed in life: taxes and death. I say there is one more thing that is for sure in life: reality is uncertain. No matter how hard you try or what you do, reality will always be uncertain. You will almost never know the outcome of any situation. So stop trying to control it and instead take the time to enjoy it.

So how do you do that? It's about unpacking control. Many of my clients come to me with what they feel is a control issue when in reality, it is a trust issue.

So follow me here as I unpack the relationship between control and trust. Everything we do is for a purpose, and we need that purpose to be fulfilled. Because we may see or know only one way to get there, we need to control the path. We fear being taken off that path as it could lead us into danger. The problem is, we don't trust ourselves enough or have enough confidence that no matter where the path goes, we can deal with what lies ahead. We need to believe in ourselves and understand that we can handle anything sent our way.

We all have a final destination in life. People with anxiety focus too much on that final destination. We need to understand it's not the destination, it's the journey that matters. *Always consider the distance travelled as growth.* Always praise yourself for growth. Well done to you.

Whatever that outcome may be, whatever the journey shows us, wherever the path leads, make the choice to learn and grow from it. Mistakes will be made, by you and by others. But there is very little that is wholly right or wrong.

Besides criminal acts or actions that offend the human rights of others, the only time an action becomes wrong is when you are unable to take responsibility for it and its consequences. Yet you continue to make the same decisions. Much like Albert Einstein's famous quote, "Insanity is doing the same thing over and over again and expecting different results," this is when people find themselves faced with the question of, "Why do these things always happen to me?" If you don't take responsibility for your actions then you will always have the same outcomes.

This is similar to the stance that *there is no such thing as a bad day. You're just not paying attention to what the day is trying to teach you,* and so you fall into a pattern of making the same mistake over and over again. And there's a kind of grim comfort in that. You develop a comfort zone or what I call are false realities, which I will get into more later on in the chapter of fear.

To stop this thought process, you need to get out of your head. And by that, I mean, observe your thoughts and take the initiative to act on them. You need to ask yourself, why did I think these thoughts and what do I need to do to make sure that it doesn't happen again. And then you do it.

Then you need to understand one small theory: savouring. This concept was created by Fred Bryant and Joseph Veroff. They describe it as "knowing and appreciating the positive aspects of life" by simply observing your surroundings and understanding they are there because you chose for them to be there. With these two understandings of we are not our thoughts and savouring, you can start to become more aware and present.

Early in helping people overcome anxiety, a woman reached out to me who had been suffering for over 20 years. This turned into debilitating pain that kept her from being able to even perform simple tasks. That transformed into agoraphobia. It had been just over two years since she'd been unable to leave her home, which she had grown accustomed to after 30 years of living there. After 2 months of working with her, I was able to get her out of the house. Daily she would go for a walk throughout her neighbourhood and often stop to visit friends during her outing. Her family was ecstatic. They all praised my work and what I had done. But I wasn't convinced I had performed my duty yet. One afternoon, on our regular session, she was explaining how much her life had changed and anticipating more possibilities in the future now that she was able to leave her comfort zone.

As happy I as I was for her being able to overcome her phobias and enjoy her happiness, I wanted to make sure it was to the extent that I thought it was. I wanted to know just exactly what she was feeling on her walks and where her mind was as she was walking every day. I had asked her how long she lived in that house for and she said 33 years. I then asked how long her neighbours had lived in their home for and she told me they've lived there for absolutely years and that one year after they'd purchased their home they all became lifelong friends. I then asked a straightforward question. "What have your neighbours planted in the front of their home?" She wasn't able to answer. And it didn't surprise me because most of us can't. All day we are focused on our destination and we forget about the journey.

Just that one simple question really opened her eyes and changed the way she went on her walks. She stopped thinking about the fact she was finally able to get outdoors, she stopped dwelling on the fact she had been harbouring herself indoor for such a long period of time, and she also stopped worrying about what if it ever happened again. Instead she focused her attention to every second of the day, by staying and focusing on the simple things that we do every day, like washing our hands and not taking the time to smell the aroma of the soap that probably took an hour to pick out while you were shopping for toiletries. She started to enjoy her surroundings and took value in everything she seen on an entirely different level. She had finally understood how to become aware. Now it was only a matter of retraining the mind to stay in that world.

Moving forward she was able to start catching herself during every task and it became a game with her. As she was brushing her teeth she'd automatically think about what she needed to do next to get herself ready for that day, and then she'd stop herself because she was finally able to realize the next step not only could change within a second but also that was never guaranteed.

"So let me focus and enjoy the current task I am

in now," she'd think to herself. And every time after she would catch herself, she would laugh and go right back into the present moment, for her life has changed on so many levels. Her health improved; her relationship with her husband, she told me, was better than the honeymoon stage, and even her business began bringing in numbers that she'd never dreamed of, all because she was able to be in a state of awareness. She was logically able to make decisions based on the current events and have the ability to come to conclusions not based on fear or the anxiety of the future, but instead from a rational standpoint. She was able to listen more when speaking with her husband and understand him better. In turn, she was able to communicate her needs back to him with a clear conscience. Together they were able to talk to each other instead of at each other, and they were able to grow as a couple and learn more about not only themselves but together as a happily married couple.

Of course not living with the pressure of constant worry from her thoughts, she was able to understand that she was just an observer of those thoughts, and in reality those thoughts were just that – thoughts. Not living with constant anxiety and overthinking, her stress (much like her chronic pain, nausea and other ailments) quickly diminished. She was getting better quality sleep and her energy levels were back to when she was a young adult.

People do not have to be suffering from anxiety and depression to miss out on life. Even people who are living life to the fullest of their abilities often question how much they also are missing out on, much like my client was. Much like myself, when I cried because I noticed how green the tree was. The thirty plus years leading up to the night of my suicide attempt, my mind was in constant thought. I was never really able to enjoy anything fully and completely, and even the very brief periods where I could enjoy life somewhat, I can barely remember them. I know it was because I was always conditioned to worry. I never took the time to value and appreciate my surroundings.

Yet we think back to past times and miss them. Most of us always want to go back in time to relive certain moments. Why? They've already happened and still happen daily. It's never too late to enjoy the ones that happen now and to keep that feeling forever in your mind and soul.

When the gun went off that night, regret instantly overwhelmed me. I was so close to death I could taste it on my lips. I felt it in every inch of my body and I was relieved when I came to and was still alive. That was the moment I became aware. For me, being present was a gift, a gift that saved my life. After that, everything I saw around me was a gift, and I wanted more and more. After that, everything I looked at I saw in a different light. Nothing seemed the same to me after that.

When I got home and noticed my son I thought about him growing up, being your typical teenager and not wanting to be around as much moving forward with his life on his journey and not needing daddy. Daddy. Just hearing that is enough to light your soul, and knowing you won't be hearing that for long is enough to want to hear more of it.

After that, my son later told me that my parenting changed. I took the time to listen, to listen to his cute little voice, every time. I took the time to enjoy every second I had with him because every second was one closer to him growing and moving forward and I wanted to savour it all.

There's not much in this life that lasts forever, and that's not a bad thing at all. In fact, it's a good thing. So we need to stop and enjoy it while it's there. Take the time and pay attention to your surroundings, value them and enjoy them. Learn from the past but be able to move forward from it.

If you cannot do so, that is because there's still something there you have not been able to have closure on yet. There is a lesson to be learned and because you have not been aware you've been unable to pick up on it. No need to worry. I can assure you, it will come up again at some point in your life. But this time you will be ready to make a different choice. Do not worry about the future, plan for it. But do not worry about it; it hasn't happened yet. Instead, trust yourself enough to know whatever may come, you will be able to handle it and learn from it and most importantly trust yourself that you will get through it.

And how do you learn to trust yourself, and release that punishing control?

Ask yourself this - How old am I? Now think about all you have been through in your life, the times you thought your world was falling apart, that you would never be able to get out of this hole you were in. Maybe a bad break up, could be the passing of a loved one, maybe even losing a job. Whatever it is that you've been through, I'm sure you thought that was the end of the world. You would never be able to get yourself back up from that moment of pain and suffering, or even confusion. Great news. You are still here reading these words, which means you have survived. So pat yourself on the back. You see, you did it.

And you can do it again.

Now you might say it was a struggle and still proves challenging. Of course. I know all too well about that pain. And if you are not able to be aware and present during this time, you may feel "stuck." Life is all about learning and growing all day, every day we are learning. But it is up to us to receive these lessons. As hard as some may be, they only become more comfortable and help us grow each and every day.

By doing that, by learning from the day's lesson and changing our perceptions, by savouring the day, by trusting our ability to make it through, you will be able to start the transition of your mindset from living in your thoughts to living in the present.

STEP TWO

Understanding Emotions

To better recognize your own emotions, you first need to understand emotions in general. Emotions are mental activity and contain a certain degree of pleasure or displeasure. Over the past decade, scientists have spent a great deal of time investigating emotions and what emotions entail has broadened and drifted to many other meanings. To this day, astonishingly, there is no consensus on a definition.

Many theorists claim cognition is a significant part of emotions. But many times we get so engulfed in our feelings because of the chemicals that are released in our body that we are not able to think clearly. The physical aspects of the chemicals take over and overwhelm us, and without being in the mental state you need to be in, those chemicals can initiate a series of events that overtake our nervous system and send us on a downward spiral. There are endless possibilities of actions that we most always regret. So I don't completely agree with the theorists who say that cognition always plays a huge role.

Emotions are in almost every circumstance you face. But an important thing to remember is how you perceive these situations. That plays a significant role on the emotion you feel. It is your thought process that will have the most significant influence on your reaction to the emotional circumstance that follows. Emotions can and should always be used in a positive manner. I look at emotions as the guide to your thoughts and if used correctly, can help you to have a better understanding of yourself and also those around you. Emotions understood through your thought process will improve communication with a more favourable result, and you will have a sense of accomplishment when you are able to have more control over those reactions to the initial emotion.

Now let us take a look at one particular emotion that I feel is a response to deep emotion – anger. Being an actor and constantly studying my craft has really helped me to open up and actually has had a significant impact on my life and influence in this book. Let me give you an example of one of the many lessons I learned from acting and living.

I was in the studio working on a short film, and in one particular scene, my character was having a heated argument with his wife. When I was going over the lines, I was writing emotions for that part (as I always do), and the emotion in that scene was anger. So our acting coach yelled out, "Action," and boy! did I go into action. But as soon as I delivered my first line, he just as quickly yelled, "Cut." He turned to me and asked, "What are you doing?" I very confusedly answered, "Acting." To which he replied,

"Yes, you are acting. Why are you acting?" I was frozen. I had no idea what he meant. He then said to me, "The art of acting is not acting."

Although I was confused, I still understood the basic fundamentals of acting. He went on to tell me on camera all he saw was an angry man and that's all the audience would also see. I had to step away and think about this for a while and then it came to me. Anger is not a primary emotion. It is a reaction to a deeper emotion. As an actor, I needed to show the audience why it was that I was angry. If I couldn't, then all they'd see was an angry man with no reason.

In life, anger has had the best of us many times because anger is the first reaction we go to. In fact, it is probably the easiest reaction to get out of most people because we use it for other reasons as well. For example, anger is full of energy; it gets you going and that feels like you've accomplished something. So it can feel kind of good. But ultimately, any good that comes from anger is short-lived. It's another distraction from the real problem that underlies the anger.

Anger can also be used as a protection. Ego and pride are two things we all have. Ego is the hardest thing to not only to admit to but to also overcome because we identify ourselves with what we believe and what we do as the right thing. So if someone has different values and/or does things different from you, that contradict you and your values, then it feels like you've been insulted. So anger then protects you from actions or values that might cause you to be more open and aware.

By having that closed mind, we are then not able to allow ourselves to have more understanding as to why others do the things they do. When we leap to having a hurt ego, when we permit our pride to be so easily bruised, then we become the only measure of acceptability. We define what is right and wrong. We are the very definition of it. And that's very close-minded. The second that anything or anyone interferes with that closed mind, anger raises its ugly head and takes over.

Anger, much like fear, releases chemicals that can also send you into a fight or flight response. In that response, there is no logical thinking and the response will just take over. The result is that you will most likely not get to the root of the problem. And then you repeat the same mistakes because you have let anger cloud your thinking.

So to me, anger is not a primary emotion; it is a reaction.

But when we are able to understand our emotions better and understand why they happen when they do, we can open our minds up to new learnings. And then we can communicate what we are feeling to others and explain why. Then the cycle is broken.

During my 30 years of suffering with anxiety and constantly fighting with everyone around me, my wife would always tell me something that was passed down from her father. "*Never let anyone control your emotions. They are yours. Only you can control them.*"

It's a valid point. Emotions are the one thing in this world you are able to control, and when we say control, what we mean is to take responsibility for them and the actions that follow from them.

While I was going through my battles, I was constantly fighting or arguing with everyone around me. Although most of the time I had good reasons, at the end of the day, they were my reasons and my thoughts. I was constantly saying, "It's not me but everyone else." I lived that way for many years until I overcame the anxiety and the thought process that came with it. Once I became aware and present, I was able to understand better it was me and only me, regardless if I thought I was right or wrong at that time.

Looking back, I realize I took a bad situation and made it worse wholly because I was very closed-minded. I needed to constantly have control of everything because I was too scared to face anyone else's reality or opinions; I was scared of what they might think of mine.

Why was I scared? Ego and pride.

They might diss me, dismiss me, insult me and demean me. They weren't. But I couldn't take even the possibility of the idea of it. Ego and pride were how I allowed the emotions to take over the reality of the situation. Instead of taking the time to understand the deeper root of the emotion I felt at the time, I often reacted to my first initial instinct. And because I wasn't in a logical state of mind, because the chemicals in my body had overtaken my physical being, I did what I felt was normal. So I reacted to the emotions by getting angry. And then I acted on the anger by being aggressive. By following the actions (anger) to the emotions (ego, pride, and fear), ultimately what I was doing was allowing circumstances to take away my power.

When you are in that state, you are left powerless. When you can't think right, the emotion that you are reacting to takes over your body. And in the end, nothing has any resolution and you are left suffering in this state of mind: anxious, angry, fearful, hurt, aggressive. I call it *emotional bullying. And you do it to yourself without even knowing it.*

Emotions are a direct result of our thoughts, and what we see or hear will influence them. Elizabeth Gilbert said it best. "Your emotions are the slaves to your thought, and you are the slave to your emotions." By always reacting and not taking the time to understand those emotions, you are only suppressing your thoughts and not allowing yourself to grow as a person spiritually. A situation that you may be faced with can leave you feeling anger when in reality you should be feeling sadness.

By understanding why you have certain reactions to the experiences you face, you will also understand why others have those reactions. It's not that great a leap.

Let's take as an example the cheating by a significant other. Typically in this situation, the emotion would be anger from the betrayal. But when your thoughts are consumed with that emotion (anger), you are not resolving anything. You are not getting any answers. And most of the time, the doors to communication between you and your partner have long been closed. Now, I am not condoning adultery but it does happen and it is a perfect example of when emotions overwhelm us. The initial response is always how or why could you do that to me? I have helped many marriages in the past and most of the time I ask the question, "What led up to it?"

Most often because of the emotional reaction, we don't ask the right questions. And that's because we are not focusing our attention in the right direction. If you are not able to be present or aware, your relationships may be one-sided and you will have no awareness of that. Unfortunately, these occurrences do happen more and more because we're living lives mostly as robots, mechanical and unconscious. So we allow these reactions to happen without any control of them, much like a cheating spouse.

Instead of looking at yourself and what led up to the betrayal, you quickly point the finger at the straying spouse as a way of protection (anger based on ego and pride). And because that reaction takes your away your own power over yourself, once the anger has diminished, you are left with nothing but the pain that came with it. No resolution. Not understanding. If instead, you had stayed in a present state of awareness during that whole time of the relationship, you could have realized the emotion of sadness of the distance between you and your partner, and have had the ability to communicate that. Then the situation could have been resolved. And that resolution was not only for that time, but also the next time when faced with a similar situation. With your experience, you would then be more prepared and handle it logically and better.

We rarely ever think deeply of our emotions. We mostly allow them to come into our body and either take pleasure in or react negatively to whatever is passing us by. We do that without any thought of why we are actually feeling that particular response.

Life is shorter than we think and it will pass by before you know it. ***Emotions are a precious asset of living. Understand them, enjoy them and most of all, use them*** to help you communicate so you are able to learn about who you really are as a person. And by doing that, you will also understand others and be able to handle situations more effectively.

STEP THREE

Understanding Fear

Anxiety is described as the irrational fear of nothing. Obvious though the need was, understanding that fear proved to be one of the most difficult steps.

Myself, indeed most people with anxiety, live in constant fear. Most of the time, we develop phobias because anxiety creates a chronic susceptibility to phobias. I know this dynamic all too well. It was a major part of my existence for most of my life. For most people with anxiety, fear is irrational and is from negative thinking – worry. When a thought enters the mind and is perceived as a danger or threat, our system immediately goes into the fight or flight response. Because there is no logical way of thinking in this state due to the chemicals released, we are not able to rationalize and overcome the fear. Instead, we are overwhelmed with the fight/flight response and try to run away as fast as we can from whatever the threat may be.

But what about the rest of the population? Almost all of us are controlled to a certain degree by fear. Some examples of this could be being unhappy at your current job and wanting to embark on a new career but too scared of walking away from a safe and secure job; or wanting to pursue a love interest but being unable to risk rejection; or maybe wanting to rekindle a lost relationship but at a loss to know how to go about doing it; or flying, public speaking, spiders, snakes, really the list is endless. It could literally be anything in the world.

This led me to thinking: does fear exist? I mean, if most people fear something different, then how is that emotion or reaction justified?

It is justified because *we fear FEAR*. The most fearful thing is the actual anticipation. Usually when we fear something, once we have actually been subjected to it or have done what we thought we feared, we realized it really wasn't that bad. So fear mainly is the unknown.

So if that's the case, does fear really exist or is it just whatever we have manifested in our own minds?

The emotion of fear is very potent and will cause your body to react in such unpleasant ways that we stay as far away from it as possible. Like most things in life, the more we avoid it and push it away from us, the more heightened and sensitive we become to it.

Living with anxiety for so long, I was the master at pushing fear away. After thirty years of it, I knew the only way to truly overcome it was to face it. We, as humans, all have comfort zones and when faced with the reality of having to remove ourselves from those comfort zones, fear is an insistent noise inside you.

And it dawned on me. In order to accomplish anything

in life, we must first attempt it.

My wife gave me great advice. She said, *"Do what you fear and the death of fear is certain."*

In order to attempt doing something we fear, we should first educate ourselves on whatever it may be. Most things we've done in life – whether it be playing a sport, enjoying a hobby, working out or achieving a diploma, starting a new job, taking a new course in education – the first time we attempted them, I'm positive the results were not what you'd expected. But the more you continued, the easier the challenges became and you were able to move forward with increasing security, gaining a higher level of accomplishment in those areas.

For me, having anxiety, I was living in constant fear. And it controlled me on every level of my life. I wanted to know why was I so fearful of so many things. And I realized for me, and I'm sure for most people, I had no valid answer as to why so many things scared me. I could write down a fear and ask myself why does this scare me? And almost every response was, "I don't know." But make no mistake that the feeling was extreme and the physical reactions were enough to make anyone run for safety, which then validated my thought of fear.

But looking more into it, I did realize so many things. One of them was that, because of fear I'd developed, I never wanted to leave my comfort zone. So this created what I call, "false realities." I made myself believe I didn't like whatever it was that I was fearful of. I needed to be in my own comfort area. My home was my safe place and I had to be within a certain distance of it regardless of where I went. I needed to have my own vehicle so not only could I control the route but also if I needed to go home, I could do so at my own leisure and not have to rely on anyone else. Living like that pushed me further into the layers of the comfort zone I'd created. It then led to me not being able to travel to more distant destinations because I would be too far away from home. I could never just go on a plane or train because I had no control and if I wanted to hurry home, I would not be able to. From there, my mind created this false reality. It convinced me I hated to travel. Although there was no logical reason for it, the emotions were so real I believed it, and did a really great job convincing others how much I hated it. Because I wasn't able to face these fears and had instead convinced myself I simply did not like to do these things, I eventually was hardly able to leave the house at all.

You do these things to survive. But you're not resolving the issues. Instead you're creating a false reality around your anxiety so that you can function. This becomes so normal, so much a part of your thinking process, that you're not even aware of it. It's like an addiction. It sneaks up on you, you don't even know that you've become addicted to these false realities. You think your behaviour is normal. When people point it out to you, you deny it so persuasively that they believe you. Creating these false realities is really running from fear, it's running from the problem, it's an addiction to surviving.

You don't want to just survive. You want to thrive.

The answers came to me when I was in a state of awareness. I looked further into the fight or flight response. For so many years, I had completely ignored the fact that the response actually had two options: fight or flight. I thought, how does this heinous feeling, this "response," allow me to fight? I got to tell you, it didn't in me. Anxiety was such an awful feeling that all I wanted to do is flight. I couldn't run away from my anxiety. So I became a control freak.

What we fail to realize is the fact that anxiety and fear are there to protect us, flight or fight is our natural form of protection. We perceive a direct threat in front of us and our mind sets off the emotion of fear, which in turn sets off the reaction, which is anxiety. And that anxiety tells our brain to release chemicals to help us better respond to the threat.

When you really think about it, most of the time there is no direct threat in front of us. *It's usually our thoughts that cause this response (anxiety to fear to flight) to activate.* Most specialists describe this as "False Evidence Appearing Real." So for the most part, it is all our own thought process that ultimately stops us from doing things we feel can pose a threat.

Some of the greatest minds in the world have said you should do one thing a day that scares you. Why? Because it helps you to grow as a person on so many different levels. You will be able to troubleshoot more effectively. You will have a sense of accomplishment. It will start a chain reaction within your system that you will want and crave more of. The end result is living your life to the fullest.

So how do we use this tool of fight/flight to propel us – as opposed to repress us? Let's look into fight or flight. This is the response that is responsible for prompting us to run in the opposite direction of fearful events and mainly it is because those events and what comes with them are of the unknown. And not knowing what to expect is why we fear them.

In the previous chapters we looked into what happens when this response is activated, and we came to the conclusion that most fears were from not knowing what the consequences were going to be. Most of the time we only fear the emotion of fear itself and not necessarily the threat. So the best way to understand anything in life is by educating yourself. You can easily use fear as a tool to help you do just that. Let me explain how.

Think about a gigantic mountain. You have seen them on many postcards and paintings across the world. Some of us may have been lucky enough to experience them close up. So look at a mountain like you would look at those obstacles in life that fear you. Take in the beauty BUT use the mystery behind it as fear. Kind of like the boogeyman. What does the boogeyman do? He preys on your weakness, and in this case, your weakness is the fear of the unknown. So how do you overcome that? Through knowledge and understanding.

So let's go back to that mountain, shall we? When you hit that mountain in life, you have many options:

1) You can just stop and not even make an attempt because of fear but where would that leave you? The mountain will always be in front of you blocking your path.
2) You can drive around it but are you really learning anything? That mountain is still there and always will be, and all that's going to happen is you will eventually run into it again, and it will only feel much bigger the next time you meet it.
3) You can close your eyes and run really fast over it but are you really learning anything about that

mountain? Why its there? What did you learn from it?

Instead, look at that mountain as one small part in your journey of life. Over the mountain is your destination. But don't close your eyes and gun your way at top speed over the mountain. Most people in life fail to enjoy or pay attention to the journey, because they are so focused on the destination.

Look, we all know ultimately what our destination is and that's death. Imagine being born closing your eyes and opening them in your casket!! Pretty sad, right? What did you learn?

So you're standing at the bottom of the mountain. Be aware. Be present. You're not climbing it yet, and you are in full control of your next decision. You're giving yourself this moment merely to take in its beauty and appreciate its existence. In that state of mind, you are able to take all of it in, as opposed to having those thoughts of climbing it run through your mind and sending you into the wrong thinking pattern you've grown accustomed to and you run away from it.

Instead, in this state of awareness, you're now able to make logical decisions. When those thoughts of fear enter, they will automatically start to make sense because you're now able to reason why they are there and take your next steps accordingly. For example, I don't have the right shoes to climb, so let me get the proper shoes I need. What if I slip and fall? Ok, so I know I need a rope to tie myself off so that doesn't happen. Or you may even say, I don't have enough experience right now so let me take a course to better educate myself before I tackle something this big. Either way, you're able to face the fear and not run from it.

Small baby steps are vital in this process, and there's nothing wrong with stopping to take a break and take it all in. Don't forget to look back at the path you have chosen and how far up you have made it because where you stand is very important. And most of all, while you take that break, take a look around the mountain and take in all its beauty because that beauty is there directly as a result of you and your accomplishment!

When you think of fear, it's automatically perceived as a negative emotion that controls people. But instead, that same fear can be used as a positive influence to overcome the most significant obstacles in life. And in all honesty, if things were that comfortable in life, would you truly be able to appreciate them to the fullest?! Fear is part of the journey. Embrace it.

STEP FOUR

Communication

Communication seems simple enough. Most people love to talk. But funny enough, it's rarely practiced properly. Communication is a vital tool in everyday living but we fail to realize how powerful it really is. It's not so much that we don't communicate, it's that we don't communicate in a way that will achieve the best results possible for ourselves. You may think because you're able to say what's on your mind and you're getting your point across that your speaking has served a purpose.

Having the ability to communicate in a fashion that benefits you is an entirely different story. As you follow the other steps and start to open up, you will notice how communicating properly can open up more doors than you ever thought imaginable. And the biggest door is right inside of you!

The very first step in communicating is to understand that whatever it is you may want to say, it's your perspective. We live in such a diverse world, in which a mix of creed and cultures sit side by side even within similar realms of society. Although people may share the same ethics and values, they have the freedom to choose their beliefs and perspectives. A brother and sister sharing the exact same upbringing and religion can have two entirely different views on life. Although they have been raised on the same beliefs, values and morals, they have the freedom to understand those codes and apply them completely differently.

There really is no right or wrong when communicating. It only becomes wrong when pride and ego come into play and your mind is so closed off to your own beliefs that you fail to hear the opposing person's beliefs. ***The beauty of life is that we are all different.*** You are unique in your own special way, and the way you were able to come to your opinions may or may not be the same way the next person has. Our differences allow us the opportunity to be ourselves and view the world how we choose to.

Religion, for example, is one of the largest platforms for debate. It can show how pride and ego are massive factors in how we fail to use communicate properly. Because of our beliefs (which typically come from how we've been raised), most people shut off their minds almost completely as soon as the subject arises. Why? We are fuelled by our ego. Our pride stops us from understanding and having compassion for other people's views.

I was raised being Roman Catholic. It is something my parents and most importantly, my grandparents, took very seriously. We would spend every Sunday in church and it was a sin to not go on religious holidays. Although both my sister and I share the same religion, we also looked at the Bible and Its messages differently. We don't always agree on each other's perspective of it. It's not a matter of how or why two people of the same blood, both raised the same way, can look at the exact same literature and come out with two different meanings from it. In my opinion, it's a beautiful thing. We were able to do that. It shows we have our own minds. We are open enough to see things differently. My wife was also raised the same as myself. She grew up with her grandparents, who were both Roman Catholic. We went to the same elementary school and in fact, we also shared the same church as children. As we became closer, we would go to church together for various occasions and she was so involved in prayer during mass that if I even said a word to the person sitting next to me, my wife looked at me like I was the Antichrist.

As we grew older, she turned to spirituality. She was into meditation and the universe and started to drift away from our Catholic religion. I didn't take that move so easily. In fact, it was a very heated argument for a long period of time. My argument was simple: "This is our religion; we are Catholic. This is how we were raised. It's our way of life growing up in an Italian family."

All I could picture was my grandmother in heaven looking down at me waving a wooden spoon, ready to cast lightning to strike me. But the fact is, I love my wife; she is everything to me. I didn't want to fight with her. I didn't want to lose that strong connection we shared and I realized that connection was because we always allowed each other to be who we really were. There were no secrets. We had the freedom to always share what was on our minds without passing judgement. In this case, I was being an emotional bully. I was not wanting to hear her thoughts on the subject because of my own beliefs and what had been nestled in my mind since I'd been a child.

The moment I opened up to her and gave myself permission to have an open mind and just hear what she had to say on the subject, I was blown away. Everything she was saying actually made sense to me. Just from having an open mind, it allowed me to actually listen to what she was saying and not just hearing her and waiting for her to stop talking so I could quickly rebut with all my points. Needless to say, I was able to learn and grow. Now I too have turned to spirituality and have never been happier.

Remember all of us think differently. We are all entitled to our opinion. So the only way we can fully be able to understand each other is with clear communication and an understanding of the other person's thoughts. I always say the best way to communicate with someone is to always put yourself in their shoes and try your best to understand where they are coming from. Keep in mind that what might not be a big deal to you, could be a huge deal to someone else. And by suppressing someone else's feelings you are not only closing the doors to communication, but the person who is trying to communicate back will start to suppress their thoughts. In turn, you stop growth and start a vicious cycle for the both of you.

So clear and quality communication is how you get emotionally involved in the conversation.

I'll give you another example. One night we were just about to sit down and have dinner when my wife called our six-year-old son to come and eat. He was playing a video game and lost his mind when he had to stop playing it. For us it was funny because we knew it wasn't the end of the world and that video game would always be there but for him. But his pain of having to stop was real and I'm sure in our past, we would have felt the same pain. But we didn't get that.

Now, there are options here. Most of us would just turn off the game and get him to eat. Some of us might yell at him to sit and eat, but is that really communicating or teaching him how to communicate properly? Instead, by calmly and patiently sitting and explaining to him the importance of eating with his family, and the fact that video game will always be there, his mind will start to open and he in turn will start communicating better himself. In time, he will realize he doesn't need to yell and freak out. All he needs to do is ask questions, knowing he'll get answers and feeling safe expressing how he feels rather than being shunned or yelled at. This leads him to trust his parents more because he understands that we, as adults, know the difference between wrong and right and the priority of eating over playing a video game.

This example goes for adults as well. When communicating, other people have been exposed to so many different situations in life that have shaped how their thought pattern works. By communicating properly, the end result will always be positive regardless if both parties agree or not. You can take away so much more from the conversation if you were able to learn about the other person's thought pattern. And for the next conversation, you'll have a more open mind.

In acting, I learned that it's not important what I say but how I say it. Say it wrong and you don't have a movie to watch. All you have is a man on screen talking about whatever it is he wants to say and he is not giving the audience any direction to follow.

You can learn so much by opening your mind up when communicating, not only about how others think and feel, but about yourself and why you have the beliefs you do. Pay attention to what the other person is trying to say and where it is coming from within them because what is on the surface may not be what is harbouring inside their soul. It's almost always something deeper within. And until you are able to put ego and pride aside, you will never know what that may be. Just as you have strong beliefs and opinions, so do others. For the most part, you may not agree with theirs or them but its not about agreeing or disagreeing. It's about learning and understanding.

So the next time you are in conversation, look at it as learning and not proving your point. And I can assure you, things will not only be seen in a different light but you will learn so much more and probably never have another argument again.

STEP FIVE

Vulnerability

By now, I'm hoping you will know that life is all about perspective and choice. Following the first four steps will help you to open yourself up to the final step – being vulnerable. I cannot stress enough how vital this is in helping you become the person you truly are and being stronger than ever before. All the other steps lead up to this one tool. It glues the other four together to change your life forever.

When you hear the word "vulnerable" the first thought people have is weakness. And rightfully so. We are programmed to think and feel what society has implanted in our minds. You always hear that positive thinking will always keep you grounded. No matter what happens in your life, you should still have a positive outlook. So why not turn tools that are deemed negative into a positive one to better yourself?

There are MANY positive points to being vulnerable. Being vulnerable means you are exposing your weaknesses instead of feeling ashamed or insecure about them. You expose them because you understand them. And if you're able to securely do this, then you can work on your weak points freely. You are also opening up your mind and digging deep into who you are by exposing everything you've been holding onto internally due to guilt or shame or embarrassment.

Children are very vulnerable, and clearly do live a very free experience when it comes to being able to grow and learn about themselves. The problem is that once we get to an age that we understand emotions better, judgment plays a factor. And we start to close up internally. We become really insecure because we are always worried about how others view us. And that's when we begin to suppress our thoughts and put on hold our hopes and dreams. And we're not just living life and just trying out new things, like we did when we were kids.

But here's the thing. The only thing that silences our dreams is action. That is, actually trying to make them happen. You can ignore them to the cows come home. They're still going to be there. They'll just be suppressed. *Dreams can only really be silenced by our actions. And we don't do those actions because of our thoughts.*

I had a client, a man in his 40s, who had been living with depression for many years. He wasn't able to pinpoint the root cause. After working with him, we figured out it all came down to one isolated incident during his early high school years. He had watched a movie with his father about a male ballet dancer and found the art of dance mesmerizing. Most of the time, we have our own reasoning as to why we enjoy things or pick up specific interests. But until we are actually subjected to this, we may never know why. In this particular case, he was never able to understand why he enjoyed it because by the time he got to school that following week and opened up about it to his friends, he was immediately made fun of. Now we can all say he needed new friends and I can agree with that. But this is the unfortunate reality in today's world. What happened next was that he felt ashamed and embarrassed. He went from being vulnerable to his friends to being put down. And he accepted that. He accepted their judgments and their beliefs and their perspectives on life. Not his. He accepted that he himself was wrong and bad, and the rest of the world's beliefs were always good. He didn't have the faith in himself to stand up these friends and tell them that they were welcome to sneer at dance but he himself, he'd keep liking it. He believed his feelings were wrong and that boys or men should not have an interest in ballet. Dance was something that should be taken up by females and men should be outside playing sports.

Believing everyone else but yourself is naïve.

Now we obviously know that this stance on dance is untrue. But to this young man, barely into his teenage years, it sent him into an unconscious downward spiral. He suppressed his desire for dance and took up sports. From there, he lived his life making decisions not solely based on his own inner self, but based on the influence of the world around him. And here's the real kicker. That world of rigid roles, he created for himself.

After we'd figured this out, he was able to go back and change his thought process of what had happened. And from there, he was able to turn his thought patterns slowly to begin to live vulnerably as opposed to being "naïve".

We have been controlled to believe that vulnerability is a bad thing and we need to protect ourselves. But in reality, all we are doing is becoming naive. Being vulnerable means being open. And of course, by being open, there is a chance you may get hurt. But by following the first four steps, you will be able to use those tools to intensely learn from those decisions and, in turn, become stronger and smarter.

Take your typical tough guy. I'm positive we have all come across one of those guys in our lives either from high school or later on in the bar phase of our lives. That one guy who thought he was the biggest, toughest, and baddest. Everyone tells him that and he believes it. He doesn't just believe it – he knows it. So he hops in the ring with a professionally trained boxer.

Is he being naive or vulnerable?

He is being very naïve. He has no experience whatsoever in professional boxing. He will end up getting hurt very badly and will also be embarrassed. Because of his pride and ego, he was naive to think he knew enough about fighting that he could stand up to professionals. Because everyone told him he was the best, he knew he was. Again, very naïve. The only good thing about that situation is he probably will think twice before he lifts his fists up again.

Now, take two professional fighters and put them both in the same ring. Are they being naive or vulnerable? Vulnerable. This is something that they have trained for. They understand boxing and all the aspects of it. And once in the ring, it is about learning how to be the better boxer. Every hard punch, though painful, is a lesson on how their opponent throws a punch or dodges a punch. In the end, one person may be knocked to the ground but they have learned a lesson in that ring with that opponent. They prepared themselves and opened themselves up to being vulnerable and were able to walk away, not suppressing their thoughts or being embarrassed but made stronger and smarter.

That's what being vulnerable can do for you. Not solve all your problems but integrate all that you have learned so that you are a better, smarter, stronger you. Being vulnerable means living with self-awareness and thoughtfulness. Being vulnerable means that the self-awareness is focused on savouring the present so that as much as possible can be drawn from it. Being vulnerable is translating thoughts into actions, through listening to yourself and others. Being vulnerable is understanding fear and then doing something about it. It's understanding anger and what it masks and then doing something about it. Making yourself open takes strength and thoughtfulness. Making yourself vulnerable, makes your whole.

CLOSING

By practicing all the steps in this book, you will become stronger and more secure and entirely capable of using your own mind to open up the possibility of living life to the fullest. Life is not perfect and I'm not pretending that it is. So there will be bumps in the road. There will be times that are tough. I'm not going to lie and pretend otherwise. But we are guilty of putting up a false front that it is perfect.

Be active in as many aspects as possible to conquer your weaknesses. There is no shame in showing weakness; it's a part of life and a huge one. So why cover it up or suppress it? Open up about it, learn about it, understand it, and then you will have the power within yourself to be that better person for yourself.

Not only that, think about the lives you can influence and ultimately change by just opening up and allowing others to open themselves up to their true selves.

ACKNOWLEDGEMENTS

I really couldn't have written this book with the support of some truly excellent people. So with my deepest gratitude, I'd like to thank **Enzo Fatica, Mario Caputo, Phyllis Caputo, Sarah Ilijanich, Melinda Meier, Amanda Shotton, Andrew Oliver, Sandie Clark, Brad Milne, Rudy Pignataro, Briana Succo, Ray Lyell, Tiziana Filice, Studio Pavas, Maria Luisa Sivitilli** and **Fernando Costa**.

To **Petya Tsankova** of **Clapham Publishing Services** for the fabulous book design and the whole team at **Clapham Publishing**, a big thanks.

It's been great working with you.

www.claphampublishing.com

A special thank you to the superb photographer, **Sarah Stewart**, who took the front cover and back cover photos for this book. You can contact her at **stewartphoto@shaw.ca**

You're the best, Sarah!

CONTACT DETAILS

Anthony Caputo is a therapist specializing in anxiety disorder and depression. He runs group meetings and also does individualized sessions.

He can be contacted at
anthonycaputovlogs@gmail.com

Subscribe to his website for news and updates from Anthony.
www.anthonycaputo.co

Or follow Anthony on Instagram at
@Antonioccaputo

www.ingramcontent.com/pod-product-compliance
Lightning Source LLC
Chambersburg PA
CBHW060401080526
44583CB00012B/426